Before You Say "I Do"

by

Bishop Joseph W. Walker, III – D. Min.

Tulsa, Oklahoma

Unless otherwise indicated, all Scripture quotations are taken from the *King James Version* of the Bible.

Before You Say "I Do"
ISBN 1-892728-15-X
Copyright © 2000 by
Bishop Joseph W. Walker III, D. Min.
9 Music Square South, Suite 321
Nashville, Tennessee 37203

Published by
PHOS PUBLISHING, INC.
P. O. Box 690447
Tulsa, Oklahoma 74169-0447
918/622-3932

Contents

1
Forgiveness

And when Joseph's brethren saw that their father was dead, they said, Joseph will peradventure hate us, and will certainly requite us all the evil which we did unto him.

And they sent a messenger unto Joseph, saying, Thy father did command before he died, saying,

So shall ye say unto Joseph, Forgive, I pray thee now, the trespass of thy brethren, and their sin; for they did unto thee evil: and now, we pray thee, forgive the trespass of the servants of the God of thy father. And Joseph wept when they spake unto him.

And his brethren also went and fell down before his face; and they said, Behold, we be thy servants.

And Joseph said unto them, Fear not: for am I in the place of God?

But as for you, ye thought evil against me; but God meant it unto good, to bring to pass, as it is this day, to save much people alive.

Genesis 50:15-20

Forgiveness means to grant a pardon, to cease to demand the penalty for a particular act. Forgiveness means ceasing to blame or to feel resentment toward a particular person or group of people. Forgiveness is a universal struggle.

Everyone has some area in their lives where they are struggling to forgive. Forgiveness is hard for those who live for God -- oftentimes because we are the ones who catch the most hell, and the very people who cause it are the people God sends us back to, to say, "I forgive you." No matter how much Word we have, all of us are in this place. When we've been scarred and are wondering why people do what they do, we wonder how we can forgive. In order for us to get what God has for our lives or to become the people God wants us to be, we must learn how to forgive.

None of us would be here today had it not been for forgiveness. Had not God looked beyond our faults and supplied our every need, you and I would not be where we are today.

It's not because we did not err. We've fallen short of the glory of God on many occasions, but God is a forgiving God. I thank God that He forgave me.

Had God not forgiven me, I wouldn't be in the position that I'm in now. You need to understand how to forgive because you can't go forward in life until you release and forgive those who offend you.

As a child of God, you represent God in everything you do and in everything you say. Regardless of how other people act toward you, don't let them cause you to act on their level. Regardless of what has happened in your life, don't let it cause you to lower yourself to their level.

A Lesson from Joseph

The things Joseph went through are chronicled in chapters 37-50 of Genesis. Joseph was favored by his father. He was hated by his brothers because of his dreams, but he had favor from God.

It wasn't Joseph's fault that he was favored. He was not to blame because his father blessed him and gave him a coat of many colors. He was able to see things other folk could not see, but as a result he was hated by his own brothers.

You do not have to necessarily do anything for people not to like you. But until you put forgiveness into perspective and let go of anger and resentment, you will not understand that God has more for your life than what has happened in your past. You will never maximize your potential. You will never be the person God wants you to be.

Joseph was a man of great character, a stalwart in the Old Testament. He was a five-star believer, and he teaches us today some valuable lessons on forgiveness. After the death of Jacob, Joseph's father, Joseph's brothers became afraid. They sent a messenger to Joseph, telling him that before his father died he left a message for Joseph asking him not to get even with his brothers because of what they had done. When the messenger came and told Joseph this, Joseph cried.

When people have done you wrong, there will come a day when they will have to answer to you. God will make Jesus' enemies His footstool. (Psalm 110:1.)

Jacob's death and the message brought back the scars and the pain. Joseph had been thrown in a ditch and left to die. His brothers had told Jacob, their father, that Joseph was killed by a ferocious animal. They actually sold him as a slave to Egyptian travelers.

After a brief time as a respected slave in the house of Potiphar, Joseph ended up in jail with Pharaoh's baker and his cupbearer. All along Joseph had done nothing wrong, yet many bad things had happened to him. At the news of his father's death, his mind was flooded with painful memories. The years of hurt came to the surface and then Joseph began to cry. He had to face it.

Face It, Fix It

You've got to face it if you're going to fix it. You've got to deal with the fact that something bad happened to you. In order to go on with life, you are going to have to face it. You cannot hide behind the curtain of your religion. Deal with the fact that you are hurting. Face it and put it in perspective.

Often the reason we end up doing things and saying things that we really don't want to do or say is because we just won't face the pain of our past. We allow things to build up to the point where we almost explode because we have so much pain. If we don't face it and deal with it, we are going to end up hurting ourselves and others as well.

Learn how to cry. Learn how to release that pain. Learn how to let that stuff out. There is nothing wrong with crying. There is nothing wrong with saying, "Listen, I've got to go through bad things, but I'm not going to wallow in it. I'm going to deal with this thing, and I'm going to move on with my life." When the prodigal son was wallowing in the hog pen, the scripture says that he came to himself. He talked to himself, and gave himself a dose of reality.

A New Perspective

Facing your pain is putting into perspective what has happened to you. In Joseph's case he had to realize that something else was at work in the lives of his brothers that caused them to do what they did. The Word reminds us, "We wrestle not against flesh and blood, but against principalities, against powers, against the rulers of the darkness of this world, against spiritual wickedness in high places" (Ephesians 6:12).

When you are angry, you must learn to focus your anger not on flesh and blood, but focus your anger on that demonic power that operates in people. If you're not careful, that same demonic spirit will get inside of you and cause you to react in ways that do not bring glory to God. If you don't face your pain, then you'll start doing the same things. Because you were mistreated, you will start fussing at everybody else. Somebody beat you so you start beating up on everybody else.

Joseph was not hurting over what his brothers did but over what they allowed the devil to do through them. The devil wants you to take it out on the person who was used to hurt you, so you both will be destroyed.

The Great Oz

Remember the Wizard of Oz? Dorothy and Toto were following the yellow brick road trying to get to the Oz. On the way they met a scarecrow who was looking for a brain, a tin man looking for a heart, and a lion looking for courage. They all trembled at the booming voice declaring, "Who disturbs the Oz?" Little Toto, the dog, started pulling on the curtain. When Toto moved the curtain back, the voice was still repeating, "Why are you disturbing the great Oz?" But behind the scene there was just a little man. He was pushing buttons, causing everything to happen.

You may be afraid and about to give up. But what you need to understand is it's nothing but a little man behind a curtain, pushing somebody's buttons. It's nothing but the devil pushing somebody's button, causing them to make trouble for you. Don't allow one behind the curtain to push your button like that. Don't allow someone behind the curtain who is pushing someone else's buttons to defeat you either.

Now once I do that, once I put that in perspective, second of all, I want you to get this, I have to avoid fellowship with the past. Avoid fellowship with the past. Look at verse 19. Notice what Joseph says.

> **And Joseph said unto them** [to those who had done him wrong], **Fear not: for am I in the place of God?**
>
> **Genesis 50:19**

In other words, they were saying, "Joseph, don't do anything to us." Joseph said, "Don't worry. I'm not God." When you put your pain in perspective, you will be able to bring glory to God in a way that represents Him. Joseph told his brothers that whatever happened in his past concerning them, he had let that go and was letting God deal with it. God can handle your past.

The Past Is Past

The past is past and there is nothing you can do about what happened. There is nothing you can do to change it. Once you have faced it, turn it over to God. Let God deal with it. If you are depressed, oppressed, suppressed and pressed, it may be because you have not let your past be past! Too many people are spiritual pack rats. Year after year they just pile it up – offense after offense – until they can't see anything good because offense is piled up all around them.

Crippled Future

Sometimes as soon as you meet somebody new, you don't trust them because someone in the past let you down. You mess up a perfectly good relationship because of what happened in your past. If that is happening in your life, then your past is defining your present. If you had a bad experience with some woman, every woman is suspect. If you had a bad experience with some man, every man is suspect. If you had a bad experience with a white person, every white person is suspect. Or if you had a bad experience with some black person, every black person is suspect.

You should never generalize things based on your past experiences. You must let them go. Let God deal with them. They are too much for you to handle. "This one thing I do, forgetting those things which are behind . . . I press toward the mark for the prize of the high calling of God in Christ Jesus" (Philippians 3:13-14).

No More Sting

This is what happens in your spirit when you let

something go: God takes the stinger out of it. Once you have been stung by a bee, every time you see a bee, you're sure it is going to sting you. You may be there right now. When you see some of the folks from your past, they sting you. Your blood pressure goes up.

When you turn it over to God, He takes the stinger out of it. So now it is nothing but a buzz. No one is afraid of a bee without a stinger. Every time you see your past, you just look at him/her/it and say, "Buzzzzzz." It doesn't sting anymore. God has taken the stinger out of that stuff. It doesn't sting anymore.

Once you have faced the facts and faced the pain, then you say to yourself, "I'm through with that. You can walk in front of my face. You can do whatever you want to do now, but that doesn't even faze me. It is nothing but buzzing."

Promises for the Future

If you're going to forgive, you have to approach your future based on the promises of God. It's Joseph's testimony. True forgiveness can only come when everything is put into its proper perspective. God has the ability to bless you through it all.

Joseph's name means *God will prosper* or *God will*

bless. In order for him to receive what God had already ordained for his life, he had to let that stuff go. God can't bless folks who hold grudges.

It is clear what the intent of the devil was. The devil's intent was to destroy Joseph all along. All of the mess was planned to destroy him. When Joseph put it in perspective, he recognized what the devil had been doing all along. Satan tried to destroy him. Satan tried to mess up his self-esteem. He tried to take every penny Joseph worked hard for. He messed with Joseph's childhood, but God was always right there leading Joseph through.

Whatever comes against you can't get across the bridge of *but God*. When you just think about all the things you've been through, you know that you are only here today because God was at work in your life. Everything was dark but God brought the light. God has a way of taking what the devil used for bad and turning it to good.

The only way God can turn it around is if you give it to Him. You've been holding onto that for a long time. It has shaped you now. The way you feel about yourself is inferior because of what happened in your past. You're walking around bitter, not feeling good about yourself or about your future because of what happened to you.

You can only experience forgiveness when you're able to put this into spiritual perspective. The very thing that the devil intended for your destruction, God can take it and use it for your good. God is able to transform what the devil tried to destroy you with into something He can bless you with.

Joseph declared, "[You] thought evil against me; but God meant it unto good, to bring to pass . . . to save much people alive" (Genesis 50:20). His message was one of forgiveness and acceptance of God's plan for his life – a greater plan than anyone could conceive.

You too can survive, regardless of what's happened in your past. Forgive, because you are a survivor. You haven't lost your mind. You haven't given up on life. You are a survivor. The reason you are still standing is because God wants you to tell somebody else that they don't have to give up on life just because of what happened in their past. God meant that thing for your good.

Therefore, you can say to your enemy, "Thank you, because I never would know how to pray had I not gone through what I went through. I never would know who my true friends were had I not met you. Thank you. I would have never known what true love was if you hadn't broken my heart." I thank God for everything I've been through because it's made me a better person.

You are more than a conqueror. My favorite scripture in the whole Bible is a testimony and it's this: "And it came to pass." The trouble is gone, the heart-ache is gone, the misguided friendships are gone, the hurt is gone. It's gone, but I'm here. I'm still standing. I outlived that thing that tried to take me out. It came to pass and forgiveness opened the door and ushered it out.

2

It's Not Over, Because You Can Start Over

And it came to pass, that, as the people pressed upon him to hear the word of God, he stood by the lake of Gennesaret,

And saw two ships standing by the lake: but the fishermen were gone out of them, and were washing their nets.

And he entered into one of the ships, which was Simon's, and prayed him that he would thrust out a little from the land. And he sat down, and taught the people out of the ship.

Now when he had left speaking, he said unto Simon, Launch out into the deep, and let down your nets for a draught.

And Simon answering said unto him, Master, we have toiled all the night, and have taken nothing: nevertheless at thy word I will let down the net.

And when they had this done, they inclosed a great multitude of fishes: and their net brake.

And they beckoned unto their partners, which were in the other ship, that they should come and help them. And they came, and filled both the ships, so that they began to sink.

When Simon Peter saw it, he fell down at Jesus' knees, saying, Depart from me; for I am a sinful man, O Lord.

For he was astonished, and all that were with him, at the draught of the fishes which they had taken:

And so was also James, and John, the sons of Zebedee, which were partners with Simon. And Jesus said unto Simon, Fear not; from henceforth thou shalt catch men.

And when they had brought their ships to land, they forsook all, and followed him.

Luke 5:1-11

One of the most disturbing attitudes believers have is that it's over. We resign ourselves to situations based upon what we view as facts. We conclude that there was nothing else that could be done. It's disturbing because we as believers of God are not to walk by sight but by faith.

One frustrating thing is to work hard at something, then what you expect from that labor doesn't come. This causes us to feel hopeless and helpless. We get the attitude that there is nothing else we can do that is going to help.

Don't let the devil convince you that just because you didn't have success on the first go-around that you have to walk away from what God has already promised you. God does not want quitters. You've got to have the God-kind of faith and determination so that it doesn't make any difference how many times you've missed a thing, you are not going anywhere until you get what you came for.

If you want it bad enough, then you will make up in your mind that you are going to do something about it. You cannot walk away from it and put your tail between your legs, or have a pity party. You must learn that everyone has made mistakes. Everyone has tried to do something that has failed.

Begin Again

Can you imagine how many times Mark McGuire struck out before he started hitting home runs, but he always came back to the plate? Can you imagine how many times Michael Jordan shot bricks before he got that perfect shot? He kept going back to the court. You've got to make up your mind, "I'm going to keep coming back until I get what God has for my life."

There is a God-ordained destiny for your life. As

long as there is breath in your body, you can start over. As long as you have the possibility of another day, you can start over.

Jesus stood by the lake of Gennesaret, and He saw two ships by the lake, but the fishermen were gone out of the ships because they were washing their nets. They had been fishing, but they caught nothing but frustration, so they were cleaning their nets; they were through for the day – giving up, hanging it up for the day.

Washing nets is a tedious process. If you had caught something it would justify going through the tedious process of washing your nets, but when you find yourself washing the nets when you have caught nothing, it seems more tedious somehow.

That is where many people are today. Perhaps you are carrying the burden of washing nets. You have done all you can do, but you have caught nothing. You have that "washing your nets" attitude at this point in your life. You may feel that you have tried to make it work – labored at it. But nothing came out of it so you are tired. You may be saying to yourself, "I'm through, I'm washing my nets. I know I'm supposed to be working, but I'm washing my nets. I'm tired of living like this. I'm tired of this living hell. I'm washing my nets."

Remember Who You Are

You are a child of God, and don't ever let the devil cause you to walk away from your destiny and start washing your nets. You cannot give up on what God has for your life. Shame on you for sitting back talking about, "I'm giving up, nothing can be done." *Man's extremity is God's opportunity*, and just when you have done all you can do, that's when you ought to turn it over to Jesus.

The men were out of their boats when Jesus showed up. This may be where you are. You have left the ship. You've left the place where God wants you. You've let frustration run you away.

We need to have the kind of faith that says, "I'm going to stay here until I catch something, because I'd rather be in the will of God, catching nothing than be outside of His will, washing my nets." The fishermen were spending more energy and time on that which represented quitting rather than using that energy on that which represented success.

Stop washing your nets. There is something else God wants you to do. You may have frustration. You haven't got what you wanted. You thought it was going to come to fruition by now. It has not but it's still not time to wash your nets.

Jesus Enters the Ship

When Jesus shows up, whatever situation you're in is going to change. Wherever Jesus is, there is possibility. Wherever He is, there is hope.

Jesus entered into one of the ships and told Simon Peter to push out just a little from the land, and then He sat down, and began to teach. First of all, Jesus got into what they abandoned – their ship, their transportation to their destiny. He got into their ship. Jesus is the Word. "In the beginning was the Word, and the Word was with God . . . And the Word was made flesh . . ." (John 1:1,14).

When Jesus got into the ship, the Word got on board. Jesus, the Word, is about to get into your relation*ship*, friend*ships*, fellow*ships* and your steward*ship* because if Jesus is not in the ship, you're on a hard*ship*.

The reason why a lot of us don't catch what we're supposed to catch – we're not successful – is because we don't let the Word come in our ship. We have everybody and everything else in our ship, but the thing that most needs to be there. You've got everybody speaking in your ship. Everybody hanging around in your ship. You need to make sure Jesus is aboard.

And when the Lord – the Word – gets on your ship, don't think it's strange when He starts pushing you away from some folk. He's pushing you away from the doubters. He's pushing you away from the negativity. What He's getting ready to do in your life, the bank folks may not understand. What He's getting ready to do in your life cannot be found on the bank. It's on the sea. Don't get comfortable on the bank. You've got to push out a little from the bank, and you've got to understand what God wants to do. It's on the water. God is pushing you away.

Whenever the Word gets in your ship, He begins to teach. The devil has tried to prevent you from hearing the Word of God, but God is raising up a people now who really want to know His Word. We have gone too long without understanding this Bible and we have gone to church and we've not gotten the full Word of God. People are getting tired of that now. They want to understand the Bible because the Word will help them make sense of their lives. My breakthrough is in the Word because I understand that faith comes by hearing and hearing by the Word of God. (Romans 10:17.)

Jesus began to teach. He didn't holler. He didn't whoop. He taught. He taught them out of what they abandoned. He brought the Word into what they had given up on. And that's what God will do for you. He will bring a Word into that thing you gave up on to let you know that you can start over. When you step out, He steps in. Whatever you step out of, He will step into. He will bring you back into it, to let you know that there is still possibility.

We can assume that Jesus taught them what they were doing wrong. It's not that the fish were not available. The problem was the method. Nothing was wrong with the fish, but what caught fish for you yesterday may not catch fish for you today. You can't catch today's blessings with yesterday's method.

Move on Out

When Jesus finished teaching, He told the fishermen, "Launch out into the deep." We assume if Jesus told them to launch out into the deep, that they had been fishing in shallow water. This could be part of your problem. In shallow water, your boat is bound to get bruised by the rocks or get stuck. If you've been trying to get your blessings in shallow water, perhaps you've gotten stuck in certain situations you can't get out of and you always end up getting wounded and damaged. Stop trying to get your blessings in shallow water! If you want to catch a tadpole, you can hang out in shallow water. But if you want the big blessings, you've got to go out into the deep.

I'm tired of shallow water blessings. I'm tired of shallow friendships, shallow relationships, shallow situations. I want the deep blessings. I want everything God has for me. I'm coming out of shallow water. What God has for me is in the deep.

There's another problem with shallow water. All the debris comes there. All the junk is at the bank in the shallow water. The deep has a way of washing it toward shore. If you are dwelling in the shallow water, you're settling for stuff that the deep doesn't even want. You've got to stay out of the junky place. You've got to stay out of the nasty place. You've got to launch out into the deep, even if you have to do it by yourself.

I want to be in the deep in my relationships. I want to be in the deep in the Spirit. I'm tired of being in shallow water. I'm tired of shallow-water people. What happens is, notice this.

The junk that gets in the middle of the sea gets moved toward the shore. The deep cannot stand the junk so it sends it to the shallow. When you get deep in God and the shallow stuff starts coming to you, you won't be comfortable around it. If you are wondering what's going on inside of you, why your spirit is troubled, why you're feeling like you're feeling, it may be because you've got too much shallow stuff around you and God is trying to tell you. That stuff will make you sick until you get away from it or get it away from you. Allow the floodtide of God's Word to wash it away to the shallow places.

Whenever God blesses you, it should lead you to worship. When God blesses you, the ultimate end of a blessing is that it will lead to worship. Praise should lead to a greater knowledge of who He is, therefore creating within you a worship for who He is. So regardless of your next situation, you're not actually responding to what He does. You're responding to who He is.

When God blesses me, He blesses me because He's trying to lead me into worship. That's why He turns things around in my life. He wants me to say thank you, but I am not responding to God based on what God does for me. But based on the knowledge of what He has done, I have gained a knowledge of who He is. So regardless of whether He does something or not, I know too much about Him to doubt Him. So I worship Him for who He is.

Simon said to Jesus, "We have toiled all night long and caught nothing." How many times have we said things like that? "I have taken this test three times and caught nothing." "This is the fifth time I have asked them for a promotion, and I have caught nothing." "I have tried to make this relationship work with him. I cook, I mow the yard; Jesus, I have caught nothing."

The Nevertheless Place

We must finally come to the place where we can say, one more time, "But nevertheless, if You say to do it one more time, it's because I know too much about You now. I'm going to do it this time. I don't care what happened on the other times. Nevertheless at Your Word, I'll do it. I'll let down the net. I'll get back in the boat and let the net down again."

When the fishermen obeyed the Word of God, they enclosed a great multitude of fish, so many that their nets began to break. One moment they were washing their nets, giving up. The next moment they had so many fish that their nets were about to break.

This is the beauty of stepping out on God's Word. He will move you from zero to more than you need just by taking Him at His Word. He has a way of sending His Word at the right time. Just when it looks like you have got nothing left, He says, "If you just take me at My Word, and step out on the water, I'll bless you in such a way that it will blow your mind."

Net-Breaking, Boat-Sinking Blessing

Whenever God blesses you, He blesses you with more than enough. The fishermen had to call to other ships to take some of the blessing or they would sink from the abundance. If you are selfish and stingy, you're going to sink with your blessing. If you keep all the fish on board, your boat is going to sink. So you've got to call somebody else, and you've got to get rid of some of it. He gives you more than enough to supply your needs, so it must have been given to you in order for you to bless somebody else. You can't stay afloat unless you bless somebody else. God has blessed me so I can bless others.

When Peter saw the miracle he fell down. Falling down at Jesus' feet was a sign of worship. And the reason we know it was worship is because in worship you always see God. He saw the act, but when he saw what God did, he knew who God was, and then he saw himself and recognized his need to repent. After he began worshipping God, everybody else was astonished, and they began to give God the glory.

So whenever God does something for you, give Him the glory. Whenever you receive a blessing, give Him the glory. When you remember that it was not long ago you were washing your nets with your lip stuck out, and now God has blessed you in a way that it has blown your mind, you need to give Him the glory.

It's not over because you can start over. God will send His Word. I know you're frustrated, but you can make it. I know what it looks like, but you can start over.

When I was in Southern Baton Rouge as an English major, Dr. Dorothy Newman made an investment in me as a professor. She said to me, "You have a unique ability to write." She told me one day to sit down, and she gave me this big, thick notebook of paper.

She said, "Sit down there, and I want you to write a poem that expresses your pilgrimage to this point." I started writing and writing and writing. As I sat there in the room by myself, I said, "Naw, that's not it," and threw the paper away. I kept doing that. She came back into the room and said, "How's it going?" Then she looked on the floor. "Well, it must not be going too good. I see paper."

I said, "Well, you know, Dr. Newman, every time I think I have it, it's not it. So I've just been starting over and starting over." She looked at my notebook and said, "Well, a good thing about it is, you've got enough paper." It dawned on me that that's how life is. You look at some of the things you try to do, and you say to yourself, "I was trying to make that work, but I blew it." Then you try something else and it goes wrong.

The world looks at your false starts and calls you a failure. But as long as you keep having a clean sheet in front of you, it represents brand new mercy. It represents a new day. So stop looking at the past. Start looking at the fact that you can start over. Stop complaining about what didn't happen. Just know that as long as there's breath in your body, you can start over. God will give you a second chance.

Make this declaration with me now: *I thank God that He gave me a chance to start over. As long as God gives me another day, I can start over. I may have messed up, but I'm starting over. I made some mistakes but I'm starting over. I'm coming out of the shallow place. I'm tired of shallow relationships. I'm tired of shallow conversations. I'm tired of shallow things. I want to be in the deep place. I've made up in my mind that when God blesses me, I'm going to bless others and I'm going to give God the glory.*

3
The Ministry of Marriage

The name of the first is Pison: that is it which compasseth the whole land of Havilah, where there is gold;

And the gold of that land is good: there is bdellium and the onyx stone.

And the name of the second river is Gihon: the same is it that compasseth the whole land of Ethiopia.

And the name of the third river is Hiddekel: that is it which goeth toward the east of Assyria. And the fourth river is Euphrates.

And the LORD God took the man, and put him into the garden of Eden to dress it and to keep it.

And the LORD God commanded the man, saying, Of every tree of the garden thou mayest freely eat:

But of the tree of the knowledge of good and evil, thou shalt not eat of it: for in the day that thou eatest thereof thou shalt surely die.

And the LORD God said, It is not good that the man should be alone; I will make him an help meet for him.

And out of the ground the LORD God formed every beast of the field, and every fowl of the air; and brought them unto Adam to see what he would call them: and whatsoever Adam called every living creature, that was the name thereof.

And Adam gave names to all cattle, and to the fowl of the air, and to every beast of the field; but for Adam there was not found an help meet for him.

And the LORD God caused a deep sleep to fall upon Adam, and he slept: and he took one of his ribs, and closed up the flesh instead thereof;

And the rib, which the LORD God had taken from man, made he a woman, and brought her unto the man.

And Adam said, This is now bone of my bones, and flesh of my flesh: she shall be called Woman, because she was taken out of Man.

Therefore shall a man leave his father and his mother, and shall cleave unto his wife: and they shall be one flesh.

And they were both naked, the man and his wife, and were not ashamed.

Genesis 2:11-25

Whenever a man and a woman come together by covenant relationship in God, there is an awesome responsibility they have to each other and to God.

Marriage is not something to be taken lightly. Too many people marry for the wrong reasons. Perhaps you feel that your biological clock is ticking. Perhaps you feel pressure of family and friends who say, "You need to go on and get married because if you don't, you're going to end up like so-and-so."

Maybe you rushed into marriage because you made a mistake and got pregnant so you felt that if you married the baby's daddy, it would make it right. Sperm donorship does not qualify soulmateship. Just because you made one mistake, don't make two.

Perhaps you met one whose resume' looked good, their bank account looked like your bank account, and you got along well together. You thought, *Hey, we need to hook up*. What happened was not a marriage, but a merger.

Perhaps you were one who loved the Lord with all of your heart. You were committed to Him and so you purposed to live holy – celibate. But there came a time when you wanted to turn out the lights and light a candle. You said, "We might as well get married because I can't hold onto all this passion." Then a few months after you released all that passion, you found there was nothing else in the relationship.

Marriage is a ministry. Marriage is not something

to be entered into lightly or unadvisedly but reverently, discretely and in the fear of God. There are some things we need to know concerning the ministry of marriage because too many people treat marriage like a magazine subscription. As soon as you are tired, you're ready to change your subscription, but real marriage is a ministry.

If you are going to appreciate the ministry of marriage, the first thing you must understand is the reward in preparation. God is a God of order. Everything God created was done in order. God prepared man before He allowed man to get married.

> **And God said, Let us** [meaning the Father, the Son, the Holy Ghost] **make man in our image, after our likeness. . . .**
>
> **So God created man in his own image, in the image of God created he him; male and female created he them.**
>
> **Genesis 1:26-27**

When God said, "Let us make man in our own image," He was talking about the spiritual nature of man. Although Adam was physically manifested first, God created the spirit of man and woman at the same time, and they had joint dominion over every creeping thing in the earth.

The word "make" comes from the Hebrew word *asah,* which means that God made something out of something that already existed. He made Adam out of the dust of the ground. But when God created the spirit, He *barahed* it. That word means to create something out of nothing. The spirit of man and woman was made out of something that did not exist.

The Lord God formed the man from the dust, something that already existed. He breathed into his nostrils the breath of life, and man became a living soul. God made man first, but only the physical manifestation of Adam. The woman had not yet physically manifested. God had put Adam's soulmate inside of him. She was already in Adam before she was physically manifested.

Perfect Placement

First, God prepared Adam by placement. The Lord God planted a garden eastward of Eden and there He put the man whom He formed. To prepare a man for marriage, God puts that man where He wants that man to be. You cannot find a soulmate who is out of place. If they will not be where God wants them to be, then I guarantee they're not going to come home when you want them to come home. God put Adam in the right place so he could spiritually prosper him.

> **And out of the ground made the LORD God to grow every tree that is pleasant to the sight, and good for food; the tree of life also in the midst of the garden, and the tree of knowledge of good and evil.**
>
> **Genesis 2:9**

God hooked that garden up. When you're in the right place and you recognize that your blessings always come from God, you won't be trying to look for somebody else to do for you what only God can do. Sometimes the problem is we want to marry somebody because we feel like we need somebody to take care of us.

Perfect Profession

> **And the LORD God took the man, and put him into the garden of Eden to dress it and to keep it.**
>
> **Genesis 2:15**

God gave Adam a *JOB*. A J-O-B. If you want a mate you need a J-O-B. Adam was not ready for companionship until he learned how to handle a job.

Perfect Procedure

After God gave Adam a profession, then He tested him on procedure.

> **And the LORD God commanded the man, saying, Of every tree of the garden thou mayest freely eat:**
>
> **But of the tree of the knowledge of good and evil, thou shalt not eat of it: for in the day that thou eatest thereof thou shalt surely die.**
>
> **And the LORD God said, It is not good that the man should be alone. . . .**
>
> **Genesis 2:16-18**

The first thing in the procedure we must learn is that God's order for procedure began with "don't touch this; don't touch that." God was trying to see how Adam could handle orders.

God exposed Adam to animals, and gave him the order to name them. Adam named them and learned a powerful lesson in the process. God wanted Adam to name them, but He also wanted Adam to recognize that he was different from the animals. God didn't create Adam to act like an animal. The problem today is, so many men are acting like animals instead of men.

Watch a tribe of lions. The male is only good in the animal kingdom for reproducing. And after he reproduces, he looks for another female in heat. God doesn't want us acting like the animals – we are to have dominion over the animals. There are some women who have animalistic behaviors as well!

We need to get ourselves together. We need to be whole before we try to marry someone. If you are not completely prepared in God, you can't look for anyone else to bring you completion. You have to be complete in God by yourself. You don't need someone else to complete you – you need somebody to compliment you. You ought to have some things together. You ought to have some things with your name on them. *You just love name brand stuff, yet you will marry a no-name person.*

Receptivity

In order to really appreciate the ministry of marriage, you've got to appreciate how God gives you a mate. The Bible says that every good and perfect gift comes from above. So no matter what my opinion is regarding a particular situation, I need to be receptive to what God wants to bring into my life.

When God was ready to give Adam a mate, He caused a deep sleep to fall upon Adam. This is the first instance of anesthesia in the Bible! While Adam slept the Lord took one of his ribs. God put Adam to sleep because God didn't need help to bring Adam a soulmate. And God doesn't need your help to bring your soulmate to you.

Sleep means that I'm not participating in the activity. The problem is too many of us won't go to sleep. You are on the Internet or running from one club to the next. You go on the love connection or dial 1-900-Singles hookup. Go to sleep. Leave it alone and let God work it out. You should know by now you aren't going to find your soulmate in a club. Leave it alone. Stop chasing after a mate. Stop looking like a fool. Just go to sleep.

When God put Adam to sleep and He opened up Adam's flesh, He released the spirit of the woman and used the rib of man to build the woman. And then God closed up the flesh for two reasons.

The first reason was to remind Adam that the woman came out of him. The second reason was that whenever God does something, He only does it one time. He closed Adam back up because there would be no need to get back inside Adam for another rib.

The rib symbolizes protection and provision. It meant that the woman would always be protected by the man and provided for by the man. When the Lord made Eve the word used for "made" was *banah*. *Banah* means to build something. When God took the rib, He began to make the woman. He built her, piece by piece. God took His time and built her. Adam was still asleep while God was building her.

Women, God is building you. He's preparing you now. God is not going to bring you incomplete to anyone. God is going to complete you first. After Eve was completely made (built) God brought her to the man. God presented her to the man, completely built.

The reason God closed Adam's eyes was because He was doing something spiritual and if Adam saw what God was doing, he might want to change some things. God was operating in the Spirit, but if Adam saw the preparation he would have been looking in the flesh. Just because someone might be anatomically attractive does not make them spiritually compatible to you.

If you just marry for flesh, that little six-ounce figure you get right now might be a two liter one day. You'd better marry one who loves you for what's inside of you and not what you look like. You need to be receptive to whomever God sends because God sends the soulmate. You may look like an odd couple but be connected in the spirit – compatible in the spirit.

The Gift of a Wife

The wife was given to Adam. You need to be careful how you treat your gift. Husbands, your wife is a gift. Wives, your husband is a gift. You need to get to the point where you understand marriage is a spiritual thing. We need to surrender our will to the will of God.

You may have been trying to put together your own mate. You have a list that you want God to use to build your mate, but you need to say, "Lord, however You want to send them as long as they are prepared spiritually and love You." You need to be thinking about the children the union is going to produce.

Final Orders

Men, go to sleep. Women, let God present you. Are you in order? You aren't ready if you're not in order. You aren't ready to get married if you're not in order. If you do not have a job – you are not in order. If you still live with your parents because you can't afford your own place – you are not in order.

If your mate does not have a relationship with God – that is not in God's order. Adam realized he was marrying someone who came out of himself. You are a new unit – your own family. When you get married, a man should leave his father and mother, and cleave to his wife so they shall be one flesh. (Genesis 2:24.)

When God chooses your soulmate – the one He has built for you – you become one in flesh and in spirit. Every marriage ordained by God is for the advancement of the kingdom, and for producing righteous seed. We must begin to see marriage the way God ordained it and allow Him to choose His best for us – for the future and for the kingdom of God.

4

True Love, Real Relationship

Though I speak with the tongues of men and of angels, and have not charity [that word means love], I am become as sounding brass, or a tinkling cymbal.

And though I have the gift of prophecy, and understand all mysteries, and all knowledge; and though I have all faith, so that I could remove mountains, and have not [love], I am nothing.

And though I bestow all my goods to feed the poor, and though I give my body to be burned, and have not [love], it profiteth me nothing.

1 Corinthians 13:1-3

We need to get a spiritual perspective of love – the foundation of the human experience. Jonathan Swift, who was the satirical author of *Gulliver's Travels*, suggested that we have enough religion to make us hate, but not enough religion to make us love. The very fact that God so loved the world and gave His only Son so that whoever believed on Him would not perish but have everlasting life is evidence that God Himself is the essence, the very nature of love. To know God is to know love. God is love and love always points back to God.

The Kinds of Love

There are different kinds of love. One type of love in the Greek is called *phileo,* which literally means brotherly love. It's that kind of platonic love. That's where we get the word "Philadelphia," the city of brotherly love.

There is another kind of love called *eros* in the Greek. We get the word "erotica" from that kind of love. It is that sensual, touchy, feeling kind of love.

Then there is *agape* love, which is unconditional love. It is not based upon my goodness or my deserving of it, but it is literally based upon a person's desire to give it to me. Agape love is the kind of love God gives to all of us.

You cannot really appreciate it until love is put into its proper perspective. A lot of what we have been calling love is not love. A lot of what we have been calling love is literally lust.

Relationships

The word "relationship" literally means the mode in which one thing stands to another. It's important for us to understand relationship because God has made us relational people. You cannot make it in this life by yourself. People need people. You need somebody. A lot of people like to think that they don't need anybody. They think they can handle things by themselves, but God did not make us that way. He made us relational beings. That's why the Bible says it is not good for man to be alone.

No man is an island, entire of himself, but every man is a part of a bigger picture so I need you and you need me. Paul said it this way: "Not forsaking the assembling of ourselves together, as the manner of some is..." (Hebrews 10:25). We must understand fellowship in order to appreciate relationships.

> **Two are better than one; because they have a good reward for their labour.**
>
> **For if they fall, the one will lift up his fellow: but woe to him that is alone when he falleth; for he hath not another to help him up.**
>
> **Ecclesiastes 4:9-10**

Solomon in his great wisdom, validated the concept that relationships are important.

The root of relationship is relate. You cannot relate if you cannot communicate. There will be no relationship without some relating.

Putting It All Together

How do relationships and love go together? A table serves a particular function. If you are hungry and you have a tray of food and you want to eat, you may see a table with old chairs. The first thing you say is, "I need a chair." You need a chair because the chair helps serve the need that you bring to the table. The chair works in relationship to the table to meet my need.

If I'm not trying to eat, I'm just tired and my feet are hurting, I don't necessarily need a table to work with a chair. All I need is a chair to serve the need that I have. When you look at your relationships with people, you have to say to yourself, "How is this particular relationship going to enhance my life? How are my needs going to be met, and how am I going to be used to meet the needs in that person's life?"

I can do badly by myself, so I don't need more burdens coming into my life. I need blessings coming into my life. Too many of us have luggage relationships – a whole lot of baggage that wears us down rather than builds us up.

Can't Have One Without the Other

The only way you can have real love is through

relationship. There can be no love without relationship. I cannot adequately love you if I do not know you. The problem is, we have not put love and relationship in their proper order or perspective. The ultimate love relationship should first be developed between you and God. When you come into a relationship with God, you have love on a level that no one else can ever understand, because there is no human being on earth who can do for you what God can do for you.

One problem that exists between males and females in love and relationships is this. The female believes that she can find love by having sex. And the male has been taught that if he says, "I love you," he will get sex, but both concepts are out of perspective. It is important for us to understand how love falls in relationship to all of the various components that Paul addresses. Paul was with the church of Corinth, a very immature church but a very religious church. Paul has to deal with them on every issue from A to Z. They were out of order.

They loved God but they were the messiest church. They gossiped too much. They were negative. Paul sent a message to them to try to help them understand how to put the love of God into its proper perspective.

We need to look at love and relationship as it relates to the work and the ministry of the church.

The gifts of the Spirit do not bring glory to God when they are not preceded by love. There is a relationship Paul says we ought to have in regard to the work of the Church. Paul said, "Though I speak with the tongues of men and of angels, and have not love, I am nothing but a sounding brass or a tinkling cymbal." If I operate in a particular spiritual area but I do not demonstrate love in my life, to God I'm just making an irritating noise. Many are engaging in spiritual activities, and going to church, but they don't have love in their hearts so they are all simply making a bunch of noise.

God wants everything we do to be in proper perspective. Everything you do needs to begin and end with love that comes from your being in relationship and harmony with God. If you have the gift of prophecy, and you understand all mysteries, you may think you've got it going on. You may feel proud that God speaks to you and reveals things to you. You may have all this faith because you have the Word inside of you. You're Bible toting and scripture quoting. You have enough Word in you that you can just speak to a mountain and it will get out of your way. The problem is, because you have no love in your heart, because you're so negative, you really have nothing.

You can bestow all your goods to feed the poor. You help folk. You help the poor. When people have a need you help them. And though you give your body to be burned or you take a lot of punches for the cause of Christ, if you do not have love, it is worth nothing.

In other words, you're catching all this hell for the sake of the kingdom. And then you're going to die and go right to hell. That's just too much hell for one person to go through. You've got to have love in your heart. And too often many people think that just because they operate in the tenets of the faith and that they're good church workers, they please God.

Often we see such contradiction in the body of Christ. The same people you see speaking in tongues and worshipping in church don't even speak to you in the parking lot. How can you sit next to somebody on the same pew full of God's love, praising Him and not even recognize your neighbor to say, "How are you doing? How was your day? How's God blessing you?"

We're living in a contradiction. We're messing folks up. Our children see us cussing each other out on the way to church. Then we get in church and tell them to sit down while we praise God. Get back into the van and go home cussing each other out. It's a contradiction. You work in the church, yet you're always negative. Stop being so mean to folk. Some of the meanest people are church folk. They always have something negative to say. They are a bad advertisement for the kingdom.

A Sad Story

Mr. Devout Churchman had died. He was a deacon at his church and at his funeral they were reading resolutions. One of the deacons got up and was talking about the deacon who had passed. He told how faithful Mr. Devout had been, how he would always open the church up, turn the lights on. "He was always in Sunday school and church. He would always clean up behind folks in the church. He had been superintendent of the Sunday school for many years. He had given his time to serve food in the homeless shelter program. He was a great man. And we are going to miss this great man."

Later, at the cemetery, Mr. Devout's widow walked up to that deacon and said, "Now I heard you say a whole lot of things today, but I was wondering who you were talking about. Because that same great man you were talking about was the man who beat me for twenty years, came home drunk sometimes, and didn't bring his check home all the time."

Too many of us are making A's in church, but F's at home. What we talk about in church should work when we get home. If what you're doing in church doesn't work in your dorm room, if it doesn't work on that campus, if it doesn't work on your job, then your love relationship isn't right. This love has to be in relationship to the ministry of the church. Everything I do within the church walls has to be in harmony with what I do on the outside.

Church attendance doesn't impress God because you'll never come as much as the devil. God is impressed when you live outside the church the way you act inside. There must be love and a proper relationship with the work and the ministry of the church.

Don't get so busy working in the church that you neglect your home. God created the family before He did the Church. Often husbands or wives won't come to church because their mate spends more time at the church than they do at home. You may be in the church shouting, but you have a sink full of dirty dishes at home. You may be attending every meeting, but your yard needs mowing.

You may be out feeding the homeless while your whole family is sitting at home saying, "What are we going to eat?" Some of you need to go home. You hang around church too much. Go home. Many stay around the church because they are afraid to go home. They are afraid to face reality.

Loving the Outside World

How does this love thing translate to folks who don't necessarily love God? It is necessary that we learn how to get along. "Can't we all just get along?"

Too many of us handle that word "love" too lightly. We don't realize what we are really saying. The nature of real love is rooted in your experience with God. So you cannot adequately say you love somebody if you've not understood the love of God. Real love is so much deeper than the stuff we call love, because there can be no love without relationship. I can't be in love with you without relationship. I can't be in love with you if I don't know you.

Just because you look good and you smell good, and you're popular, I cannot allow myself to believe that is love. If you've been so lonely for so long, the first one who comes along that treats you right, you'll convince yourself that God sent that one to you. And God might have just sent this person into your life to be a blessing through a season, not as your life mate. You cannot interpret your love out of your desperation for love.

I want you to get to know God's love because if you get to know God's love, you'll never be desperate. You'll never be saying stuff like, "Well, my biological clock is running out. It's getting late in the evening. The sun is almost setting." So you're willing to settle for last-chance Johnny.

Paul reminds us that love suffers loooooong. You know when you come down to the altar and I'm vowing to love you and you're talking about for better or for worse. When we marry you, baby, that's forever. That's a looooong time. And in that forever, there's going to be some stuff you're going to have to deal with. You are going to realize their imperfections and then the person you're in love with will realize your imperfections. Then you are going to have to deal with your imperfections together and that's some long-suffering. Love suffers long.

Love is kind. Love is not bitter. Love encourages somebody. Love doesn't tear you down. Love gets the door sometimes. Love cooks. Love takes out the trash.

Love is not bitter and negative, and so many are so negative that folks turn away from them.

Love does not envy. It does not always want what somebody else has. Love doesn't do that. Love says, "I'm so glad for you. I'm so happy you got the promotion." You don't trip because a friend makes more money than you.

Love is not arrogant. It does not draw attention to itself. Love is not puffed up, but love builds up. Love does not behave itself unseemly. Love always thinks about how it's going to act. Love doesn't act on emotion because when we act on emotion, our behavior might not represent God in the best way.

There are some things you used to do before you really knew love. You cussed some folks out. Love does not seek its own. Love is not selfish, always thinking about self, but we've been taught to be self-centered.

As little children, we are taught to pray, "Now *I* lay me down to sleep. *I* pray the Lord, *my* soul to keep. If *I* should die before *I* wake, *I* pray the Lord, *my* soul to take." All we've been taught to think about is *I, me* and *my*. Don't touch *my*. Stay away from *my*. You'd better get your own, because this is *mine*.

Love is not easily provoked. It takes a whole lot to

upset real love. You need to talk to some folks who have really been through some things. It takes a lot to get on love's nerves. Love does not think evil. Love doesn't sit around thinking about how to get back at somebody. Love rejoices not at iniquity. Love does not rejoice at sin.

Love is going to always tell you the truth. You want to know who really loves you? It's not the folks who always pat you on the back. The folks who really love you are the ones who will call you on the phone and say, "I want to talk to you about something. You are about to hurt yourself and I don't think you should be doing that." That's real love because love will tell you the real deal.

I don't need people in my life to feed my ego. I need people who will tell me the truth. People who are always feeding your ego usually have a motive. They're usually trying to get something from you so they make you feel good to get what they want.

Love covers another's sins. It doesn't tell everybody about it. The reason why you've never known love like you should is because you're scared to talk to folks because the moment you tell them it will be all over town. That's why you really know the love of God covers you. I thank God that He does not expose me.

He loves me so much He bears all things, He covers, keeps me covered.

Love also believes all things. Love never gives up. Love believes that you can make it. Love is always the encourager. When everyone else says, "You can't do it," love says, "yes, you can."

Love also hopes all things and endures all things. Love is not just one way, it is reciprocal.

Love is not making a fool out of yourself. Sometimes there is a contradiction. We take this scripture and we say the reason you ought to stay in a bad situation is because you should endure all things. But love never intended for you to stay in a situation where you're being beaten or abused in other ways. That is not love. That's crazy. You must put love in its proper context.

Supreme Submission

In Ephesians 5, we read about husbands loving their wives and wives loving their husbands. That is reciprocal love. We must love as Christ loved the Church. Christ does not abuse the Church. Because He loves the Church the way He does, the Church doesn't mind submitting to Him. Submission is not a bad thing when you're being loved that way. When you're being treated like a queen, you don't mind submitting to the king because you know he respects you and honors you and cares for you.

However, if you're getting your head beat in and you're scared to go home, you need to get out of that situation. Get some help and let him get some help. Don't stay around and get beaten up in the name of Jesus and mess your children up. If you do, they're going to be meeting somebody whom they will allow to beat them up.

Love has to exist in order for there to be a healthy relationship. Agape love is the kind of love that God has for me. So when I realize that everyone has short-comings, I can love everyone because I realize I have shortcomings. The closer I get to God, the more I come to understand love. So the closer in my relationship I get to God, inevitably I'm going to see more of myself. I begin to see how messed up I am. I stop looking down on everybody else thinking they're not worthy of love.

I even have to love folks who are my enemies. You have to love them in Jesus' name because you are a child of God. I know that eventually if my enemies see enough God in my life, it might change their life. We must learn how to love those who have despitefully used us. I can love you because I love God. How can I love God whom I've not seen and hate my brother whom I see every day? (1 John 4:20.) When you get in the Spirit you will love black folks, white folks, red folks and yellow folks. We must get away from the color line thing because the love of God is color-blind.

Love Is Your Witness

The way in which I love God is my witness. Real love is so tied to God that it never fails. Paul said, "Love never fails." Everything else that we know will pass away and our love will be all that we can take into eternity.

Our love for humanity ought to be seen in our love for divinity. I love God too much to act the way I act, or act the way I see some folks act. My witness is tied to my relationship to God. When I'm in relationship with God, He is where a healthy relationship comes from. Whenever I'm in relationship with God, I'm always going to grow. Any relationship I get into, if I'm not growing, it is not healthy. If it's not healthy, it's not of God. Too many of us get in a relationship and it's stagnant. If God is in the midst of it, it's going to grow. It's going to prosper.

When I was a child, I spoke like a child, I understood as a child, I thought as a child, I was just like a big baby. I had to have my way. When I didn't get my way, I pouted. I whined. I kicked. I screamed. And I always needed something to pacify me. But when I matured, I put away childish things. (1 Corinthians 13:11.)

Every day we should be growing in our relationship with God. We spend too much time developing other relationships and the one that really matters, we put on the back burner.

If we are going to have successful earthly relationships, we must first understand real love, then consistently develop and mature in our relationship with God.

5

A Haircut from Hell

Then went Samson to Gaza, and saw there an harlot, and went in unto her.

And it was told the Gazites, saying, Samson is come hither. And they compassed him in, and laid wait for him all night in the gate of the city, and were quiet all the night, saying, In the morning, when it is day, we shall kill him.

And Samson lay till midnight, and arose at midnight, and took the doors of the gate of the city, and the two posts, and went away with them, bar and all, and put them upon his shoulders, and carried them up to the top of an hill that is before Hebron.

And it came to pass afterward, that he loved a woman in the valley of Sorek, whose name was Delilah.

And the lords of the Philistines came up unto her, and said unto her, Entice him, and see wherein his great strength lieth, and by what means we may prevail against him, that we may bind him to afflict him: and we will give thee every one of us eleven hundred pieces of silver.

Judges 16:1-5

I believe each one of us possesses many strengths. Each of us has certain strengths and weaknesses. But just because you are strong in one particular area does not give you a license to judge someone else who might be struggling in the area where you are strong.

The Bible says, "Judge not, that ye be not judged. For with what judgment ye judge, ye shall be judged: and with what measure ye mete, it shall be measured to you again" (Matthew 7:1-2). We each have some struggles.

Strengths and Weaknesses

The Bible teaches us that Samson was a man of phenomenal strength. And like many of us, wherever we're strong, we don't mind letting people know. The paradox of Samson's life is that his weakness caused him to lose his strength. His weakness caused him to forfeit his strength. The devil is after your strength.

Delilah cut Samson's hair, which was Samson's source of strength. Delilah was drafted by the devil to cut Samson's hair. I've come to tell you, the devil is after your strength. He's coming to cut your spiritual hair.

Samson thought he was going to get some TLC, but he ended up with a haircut from hell. I'm not talking about physical hair, I'm talking about a spiritual reality. You can hear Satan's clippers coming up in your life, and you know he's trying to take you out. He's trying to cut you down. Anyone who is destined for promotion, anybody who is moving to new levels in their life, get ready. The devil doesn't like you. He wants to take you out. And one good indication to know when you are nearing a blessing is, you will hear the clippers coming. You will hear it on your job. You will hear it at school. You will see how the devil is trying to cut you up.

I've made up in my mind I'm not going to let the devil take me out. I'm not going to let that devil rob me of what God has for my life. The Bible says that you are more than a conqueror. (Romans 8:37.) The devil is defeated. (Colossians 2:15.) If you're going to be successful in life, you've got to figure out what the devil is up to. Satan is not concerned about the stuff that you haven't started. The devil wants to bring you down. The devil wants to feed your deficiencies.

Whenever we have a weakness, we will often be guided by that weakness. In Samson's case, his weakness was women. It may not be women with you. It may be men. It may be liquor. It may be drugs. But everyone has a weakness of some type.

What is your Delilah? All of us have a weakness. The devil knows that we must constantly feed our deficiencies in order to give them power. This is a universal struggle. It doesn't make any difference if you're black, white, rich, poor, educated, illiterate, tall, short, big or little. All of us have deficiencies. We have voids, and we often use Christianity as a curtain to cover our voids.

If you are trying to use the church to cover your voids, you're going to be in the closet. You need the Lord to deal with your issues.

> **Blessed is the man that endureth temptation: for when he is tried, he shall receive the crown of life, which the Lord hath promised to them that love him.**
>
> **James 1:12**

When you are in relationship with God, you are able to deal with temptation in ways you never thought you could.

> **Let no man say when he is tempted, I am tempted of God: for God cannot be tempted with evil, neither tempteth he any man:**
>
> **But every man is tempted, when he is drawn away of his own lust, and enticed.** [That's an issue. See, it's old stuff that draws you away and then it draws you to where you can be enticed or convinced to do it.]
>
> **Then when lust hath conceived, it bringeth forth**

sin: and sin, when it is finished, bringeth forth death.
[The wages of sin is death, but the gift of God is eternal life.]

Do not err, my beloved brethren.

Every good gift and every perfect gift is from above.

James 1:13-17

When you receive something, you want it to be something that God sent you, not something your lusts drew you to. Deficiency gets hungry, and it has to eat something. That's why a child of God needs to feast on the Word of God. We've got so many people that go to church just to be going. We come to see who's there and who is not there. They come to see what the choir's going to sing.

We must get to a point of hunger for the Word of God, because when you begin seeing your deficiencies, the Word of God will begin to deal with that area in your life. That's why the devil doesn't want you to hear the Word. That's why you always get tired and sleepy when the preacher gets up.

You don't want to hear the Word because Satan knows when you get the Word of God on the inside of you, it's going to starve your weaknesses to death. Whatever you feed is going to get strong. You are what you eat. If you're feeding yourself the Word of God, you're going to get strong. If you are wondering why you are still struggling, it is because you spend more time in front of the television.

While you are struggling with your deficiencies, your enemy is jealous of your strengths. Samson had some haters, and there are some people who don't like you. They don't even know why they don't like you. They just don't like you. They make up stuff about you.

Someone Is Watching

The Gazites were watching Samson's actions. They laid wait for him all night in the gate of the city. (Judges 16:2.) They kept quiet. They didn't want Samson to know they were there. In the New Testament there was a woman caught in the act of adultery. Just like the man of Gaza, there were men watching her.

There's somebody watching you even when you don't think so. You better be careful what you do and who you do it with.

And Samson lay till midnight, and arose at midnight, and took the doors of the gate of the city, and the two posts, and went away with them, bar and

all, and put them upon his shoulders, and carried
them up to the top of an hill that is before Hebron.

Judges 16:3

Samson saw them waiting. He had so much
strength that he broke out of there and took all of the
doors of the gate and the posts with him. You've got to
make up in your own mind to feed yourself the Word
because you know you have to starve your weakness
and feed your strength. Whatever struggle you have,
there's something in the Word that can help you deal
with that area of struggle.

You can do all things through Christ who
strengthens you. (Philippians 4:13.) When you begin
feeding yourself the spiritual things, you'll grow strong
in that area and you won't be sitting around thinking
that you're not going to be anything or that you can't
have anything. You will remember the Word says, "My
God shall supply all of my needs according to His riches
in glory." (Philippians 4:19.)

Feed yourself, "O taste and see that the Lord is
good..." (Psalm 34:8). "Thy word is a lamp unto my
feet, and a light unto my path" (Psalm 119:105). The
devil wants to feed your deficiency, but you need the
Word to feed your deficiencies.

Devilish Decoys

The devil always uses a decoy. Samson first went in with a harlot, then afterward, he loved the woman named Delilah. We often go from one bad thing to another bad thing. If you don't deal with your issues, you will always think of someone else, jumping from one relationship to the next relationship. You need to cry out to God like David did, "Create in me a clean heart, O God; and renew a right spirit within me" (Psalm 51:10). Cry out to God and get in right relationship with Him. Why don't you just fall in love with Jesus and let Him bring you who you're supposed to be with?

If you have some deep issues, some deep voids and deep pains, you think that changing relationships is going to make your void go away, but the void is deeper than people. It's got to be worked on by God, from the inside out. You must take adequate time with you and God and let Him deal with you.

There were men who wanted to see Samson fall. There are people who talk to you all the time, who smile in your face, who might even come to your house, ride in your car, but they really want to see you fall. You have to always protect yourself against the "see there" committee. You have to live your life saying, "I'm not giving that committee anything to say about me."

66

These men knew what Samson liked and they used Delilah as the decoy. Whenever you expose your struggles to the enemy, he will take you out. You've got to be careful who you share your struggles with. Some of you are telling people what's not right in your house, and those same people are trying to get in your house.

Delilah was drafted. She was put up to it. She represented something that Samson liked. The Bible said, "Samson loved her." Because Samson had never been in a healthy relationship, nor had he dealt with his deficiencies, he thought he was in love. But what he loved was actually what he thought Delilah could do for him. He thought that Delilah could bring him wholeness.

Some of you are in love with decoys. You think Jack Daniels can drown your troubles away. You think reefer can cause you to rise above your trouble. You think you can go out and just party your trouble away, but those are decoys. Be careful of decoys.

Delilah was paid to take Samson out. How are you going to love somebody the devil has drafted to take you out?

You can only really love someone who has been purchased by blood. You need to love someone who has been purchased by blood. Decoys look good, but they are a setup. Everything that looks good isn't necessarily good for you.

Detecting Decoys

There are some things about decoys you can always detect. They're always attractive and they are always attentive. Delilah had it going on. The devil is an expert in presentation. Whatever you're struggling with, the devil isn't ever going to send you the low end. He's gonna send you the high end.

But here is the problem with Delilah, as is always the problem with decoys. It's cosmetic but it has no content. It looks good, but when it opens its mouth it has no substance. She seemed sensitive to Samson's need. She paid attention to Samson. She was always there. Her attention started feeding his deficiency. She was good for his self-esteem.

Isn't it strange when you try to call your prayer partner that they're out of town or they're not there? But when you call trouble, whatever the time, trouble is always available.

Samson was struggling with being by himself. He was afraid of being by himself, he could not deal with loneliness. There are many people who cannot deal with loneliness. You can't stay home by yourself and just be by yourself. You've got to go outside and walk the cat, or get on the phone, because if you have thirty minutes by yourself, you become afraid. You are afraid that you will have to reflect about your own issues. That's why you've got to always build a fire with somebody. You've got to always be with somebody. The problem is that you are afraid of yourself. When you really turn yourself over to Jesus, you'll have someone walking in the mall with you. You'll have someone sitting in the movie with you.

Delilah was audible. She kept communicating with Samson. She kept pressing him day in and day out for the secret to his strength. The root word for "addiction" is *diction*. It means to speak, to talk. That's what an addiction does. It just keeps talking to you. You get in your car and it talks to you. All night long it will talk to you.

Delilah fed his self-esteem. She fed his ego. She made him feel validated and worthy, and all along it was a decoy to bring him down. It's like putting bait in the water, knowing a fish is going to bite it. But it's a hook.

The devil doesn't destroy you right away. He does

it on the installment plan. You need to watch out for decoys. I don't know about you but I'm tired of fake people in my life. I want the real thing. If you can't be real, I don't have time for you. If you can't be in my best interest, I don't need you in my life. We need some real people in our lives, not decoys.

We have a choice to have demise or deliverance. Every believer has a choice. In the creative narrative of Genesis, God put that in motion. He gave mankind a free will – the ability to choose for ourselves. Every day as you wake, God votes for you. The devil votes against you. You break the tie.

Throughout the Bible people made choices and got out. Shadrach, Meshach and Abednego got out. Daniel got out. The prodigal son decided to climb out of the hog pen and go home. Samson didn't make the right choice. He was a victim of his own weakness. We can use Samson's life as a lesson so that we won't make the same mistakes he did. We don't have to crawl away from our situation with a haircut from hell.

Principles for Choosing Right

Number one, *you have to stop playing.* Now Samson's problem was that he kept on playing with fire. He just kept playing with Delilah.

> Can a man take fire in his bosom, and his clothes not be burned?
>
> Can one go upon hot coals, and his feet not be burned?
>
> Proverbs 6:27-28

If you keep playing, you're going to get burned. You've got to get to the point where you start taking life seriously and start thinking about the choices that you make. When I was a child, I acted like a child, but when I became a man, I put away childish things. (1 Corinthians 13:11.) You've got to stop playing with your life, and stop playing with other people's lives because you will ultimately pay the price for your foolishness.

Number two, *be careful where you position yourself.* Be careful where you're going. Samson allowed Delilah to get too close. He knew he had a problem with women, but he put himself in a position where he could fall. He ended up laying in Delilah's lap.

> Blessed is the man that walketh not in the counsel of the ungodly, nor standeth in the way of sinners, nor sitteth in the seat of the scornful.
>
> But his delight is in the law of the Lord; and in his law doth he meditate day and night.
>
> Psalm 1:1-2

71

The Lord orders the steps of good men. (Psalm 37:23.)

If you press off of alcohol, don't go hang out by the liquor store. If you press off of drugs, stop hanging out with crack heads and stop going around the crack house. If the Lord has delivered you from that ungodly relationship, why are you still paging that person? Why are you still going over to see them? Ninety percent of your deliverance has to do with where you put yourself. That's why you've got to be careful where you're going.

The Bible teaches us that we can run free from sin. Run from it. Don't be running to it. *Run* away. There is no need trying to convince yourself you're going to be strong. Just run.

I tried it for myself. There are some things you cannot put yourself in. You've got to just say, "Look, excuse me, I've got to dismiss me. I've got to dismiss you. You go your way. I'm going my way. May the Lord God watch between us while we're absent from one another. We just can't roll like this."

Number three, *you need to pray.* Samson prayed when the bottom fell out. When he messed up, he started praying. "Oh, Lord, help me. I messed up. I've fallen, and I can't get up." We always pray when we have messed up. We've gotten to a point where we just operate in praying prescriptive prayers.

We need to start praying some preventive prayers. "Now unto Him who is able to keep me from falling." (Jude 24.) "Lord, I need You to put a hedge around me. I need You to let me know who's good for me, what's bad for me. I don't want to hit rock bottom. I want to pray while everything is going well. I'm praying that You will protect my money, my life, my family." You've got to be prayed up. Ask God to give you strength, because there is protection in prayer.

When you pray, God will dispatch angels around you. You'll have angels walking around you all day. When you talk about "no weapon formed against me" (Isaiah 54:17), you're right because you're prayed up. You've got protection. God won't let certain things get near you.

Sometimes you need to get in the presence of God and be quiet so you can hear from Him, so He can show you who or what He has for you. He can show you who's against you. So many of us are in such a hurry. You've got to take your time and hear from God.

It is time for us to start praying preventive prayers. That's why I don't want just anyone praying for me. Don't let just anyone pray for you. The Bible says the effectual, fervent prayer of the righteous availeth much. (James 5:16.) There is no telling what demon might be transferred to you. Make sure those who are praying for you know how to pray – that they really know the power of intercession. You've got to have folk who really know the Lord praying for you.

Samson was strong but not in the right areas. He depended on his physical strength, but he found out that that wasn't enough. You may be strong financially. Others are powerful socially, people recognize you wherever you go. You may be powerful academically – super smart. You may be powerful relationally – everyone likes you and everyone wants to be around you.

You may have a powerful gift area. No one can do anything better than you. You're good at what you do and you have power. But you don't have power in your heart, will and emotions.

If you think *power* alone can make it, ask the White House. If you think power on earth can do it for you, ask O.J. The Bible says only after the Holy Ghost comes upon you will you have power. (Acts 1:8.) You have depended on your physical strength. You need to depend on your spiritual strength. "Greater is He who is in me than he who is in the world." (1 John 4:4.)

A Vehicle of Power

A friend of mine recently got a great new truck. He took me by the dealership to look at one for me. There was the truck in the middle of the showroom floor. I jumped up in it. The truck was black and chrome, and it had a television, a navigator system and phones in it. It was beautiful and expensive. It cost seventy thousand dollars. It was a powerful truck. There was a big book sitting in the front seat that told about all the power in that truck. It looked good with its tinted windows.

I said, "Well, let me crank it up," so they got the keys for me. I turned the key in the ignition, and nothing happened. The salesman became frantic. He didn't know what the problem was. He looked around and said, "Oh my God, what's going on?"

I said, "Why don't you pop the hood?" He popped the hood and we saw that there was no battery. The seventy thousand dollar truck would not run without a seventy-five dollar battery.

I don't care how much money you have. I don't care how good looking you are. I don't care how fine you are. I don't care how many degrees you have. I don't care where you live or what your momma and daddy's names are. It does not matter what you have in life. You are nothing unless you've got power deep down on the inside of you.

God will give you power over your problems. Power over trifling people. Power over your finances. Power over sickness. Power over disease. He will give you power. I need more power in my life. I'm tired of making the same mistakes. I need power. I need power on my job, power at school – power everywhere I go.

The only way to avoid the haircut from hell is to get the power. The power of God living inside you will spare you from Satan's sheers.

6
I'm Struggling

For we know that the law is spiritual: but I am carnal, sold under sin.

For that which I do I allow not: for what I would, that do I not; but what I hate, that do I.

If then I do that which I would not, I consent unto the law that it is good.

Now then it is no more I that do it, but sin that dwelleth in me.

For I know that in me (that is, in my flesh,) dwelleth no good thing: for to will is present with me; but how to perform that which is good I find not.

For the good that I would I do not: but the evil which I would not, that I do.

Now if I do that I would not, it is no more I that do it, but sin that dwelleth in me.

I find then a law, that, when I would do good, evil is present with me.

For I delight in the law of God after the inward man:

> But I see another law in my members, warring against the law of my mind, and bringing me into captivity to the law of sin which is in my members.
>
> O wretched man that I am! who shall deliver me from the body of this death?
>
> I thank God through Jesus Christ our Lord. So then with the mind I myself serve the law of God; but with the flesh the law of sin.
>
> **Romans 7:14-25**

I am certain you desire to be all that God wants you to be. It's that motivation that keeps you going to the house of the Lord. The fact that you are trying says a lot about your commitment to live according to the will of God. I believe if there is one thing that we all have in common, regardless of our backgrounds, regardless of our level of spiritual maturity or our position in life, is that we all have a struggle. If you are breathing there is a struggle going on in your life.

You Have a Struggle

I don't have to follow you home. I don't have to eavesdrop on you. I don't have to tap your phone. Even those of you who prophesy or speak in every tongue there is, have a struggle. You can have a Bible as big as a ghetto blaster and a big cross around your neck, but you have a struggle.

For some it's one area, for others it's another. But the truth of the matter is that there is something keeping us from being all that God would have us to be. If we could just get that one area of our life together, we would be victorious. Paul said something in an expose' of his own life. Paul was anointed and he had position and prestige, but he was honest when he said that he was struggling.

There are some things that we struggle with that we need to get some help for. There's no need of our acting like we don't have a struggle because I believe that if we're going to really help someone else, we might as well come off our own little pedestals. We need to honestly let people know that most of the things they're struggling with, we have the same struggles. You need to learn how to deal with the struggle, because if you don't know what's causing the struggle, you're going to be frustrated in the struggle.

Like Paul, our carnality is in conflict with the law. Paul suggested that it is in conflict with the law since the law (the Word of God) is spiritual, but we are carnal, we are flesh. The flesh has difficulty lining up with the Word. Carnality is opposed to spirituality.

Carnality Conflict

My carnality is in direct conflict with the law. The very things that I should not do, my flesh has the greater appetite for. The Word requires me to live in direct opposition to my fleshly reality. Therefore, it creates tension between my carnal nature and my spirit. My flesh and my spirit are constantly in contention with one another. What my body likes, the Bible says I can't have. And the devil knows it. The devil knows that unless I get into the Spirit, I'm going to live a life of frustration and letdown. That's why he wants to keep me in the flesh.

If you're going to resolve a conflict, you're going to have to do it in the spirit. There is no way that you can do it in the flesh. People who follow the Bible understand spiritual obedience so when my flesh rises up, I've got to realize that my weapons are not carnal but are mighty through God. They're spiritual to the pulling down of strongholds, bringing into subjection those thoughts and things under the law of God. (2 Corinthians 10:4-5.) That's why you have to study this Word. That's why David said, "Thy word have I hid in mine heart, that I might not sin against thee" (Psalm 119:11). My flesh can't fight it but in the Spirit, in the Word, I can do it.

Crucify Carnality

That's why I've got to crucify flesh. Paul said, "I die daily" (1 Corinthians 15:31). When I get me out of the way and get into the Spirit, then my entire life hinges on this Word. I can't make decisions without this Word. I can't date someone without this Word. I can't marry someone unless it lines up with this Word. I can't take a job unless it's in this Word. "In him we live, and move, and have our being..." (Acts 17:28).

Paul shared that his character was in contradiction to his lifestyle. His struggle was a constant vacillation between what he wanted to do and what he knew he should not do. Paul went back and forth. Plato said that the human personality is like a chariot with a two-headed horse, each horse wanting to go his own direction. Martin Luther King, Jr., said that we're all somewhat schizophrenic, constantly wrestling within ourselves, having a civil war going on in our morality.

The issue is this: What I do does not always define who I am. There are some things that you and I struggle with, Paul says, and some things that I find myself doing that really aren't me.

Now then it is no more I that do it, but sin that dwelleth in me.

For I know that in me (that is, in my flesh,)

**dwelleth no good thing: for to will is present with
me; but how to perform that which is good I find not.**

Romans 7:17-18

I know what I should be doing, but nobody ever
taught me how to accomplish it. One thing we've got
to be careful about is allowing a mistake to define a
person's character. There are a lot of things we slip into
that don't necessarily speak to who we are as a person.
If you've ever made a mistake, you know how wrong
it would be for that one mistake to define who you are
as a person. There may be some things you've done
in your past that really weren't you. Was that you tip-
ping or was it the sin in you? Paul was honest about
the fact that he had some habits that he was struggling
to break. And no matter what his heart said, his habit
said something else.

Is your habit's *yes* louder than your heart's *no*? The
Bible says, "Where your treasure is, there will your heart
be also" (Matthew 6:21). The devil wants you to make
investments into your habits because every deposit in
your habit is a withdrawal from your heart. If I'm
going to bring continuity between my character and my
lifestyle, I'm going to bring consistency between my
heart and my habit.

Paul said, "For I delight in the law of God after the

inward man" (Romans 7:22). My problem is not the outer man. I know how to put on a front. I know how to hinge theological phrases together and sound religious. I know how to act and dress the part and look like I've got it going on. My problem is not the outer man. My problem is the enemy. You can dress up on the outside, but be dirty on the inside.

Laundry Lesson

When I was down at Southern University, I remember having to wash clothes for the first time in my life, and I put all my colored clothes and white clothes in the same washing machine. I turned it on and went to play basketball. And while I was shooting basketball at the gym it dawned on me that I didn't put any detergent in the washing machine. So when I came back, my washing machine was pushed out further than the others, the unbalanced load sign was on.

I noticed something about my clothes. My clothes went in dirty, and while I was playing basketball, they had been tumbling. When I came back to get them, they were still dirty. But they were wet now which meant they were heavier than they were before I put them in there.

There are some people who come to church and just tumble but when they leave, they are just wet, heavier than they were before they walked in, and still dirty. You must apply the cleansing power of God's Word and allow it to work as you agitate. Allow God to create in you a clean heart and give you a right spirit. Let him purge you with hyssop and wash you so you will be whiter than snow. (Psalm 51:7.) What can wash away my sin? Nothing but the blood of Jesus.

The Conflict Cure

The cure for my condition is the Lord. If we're ever going to get help for our situation, we must first acknowledge we need help. Stop pretending, face up to it, you need some help.

Many of us are ashamed to own up to our weaknesses, but the only way we're going to get better is to first acknowledge that we've got a problem. Paul summed up the struggle by saying,

> **But I see another law in my members, warring against the law of my mind, and bringing me into captivity to the law of sin which is in my members.**
>
> **Romans 7:23**

My mind controls my members. You know, your

members, your active and inactive members. This warfare is mental. Our mind is the battleground for the struggle. There are some subliminal issues that create tension in our lives you may be struggling with. There is no need to expect Jerry Springer to deal with it. No magazine article can fix it.

The church has to face up to the reality there are some people who struggle with sex. Here is the struggle. It is not physical as you may think. It is mental. You can be physical while your mind is someplace else. And, you've had some mental experiences that you weren't physically present for.

If you're not careful, the devil will have some of your mental experiences to be better than some physical ones. Some of you are having relationships in your mind with folk you haven't even met. You have already engaged in it because you have given mental energy to it.

> **Ye have heard that it was said by them of old time, Thou shalt not commit adultery:**
>
> **But I say unto you, That whosoever looketh on a woman to lust after her hath committed adultery with her already in his heart.**
>
> **Matthew 5:27-28**

Paul was honest about his condition. He recognized

the anointing on his life and yet he called himself a wretched man. Paul was honest with himself. It is time for us to better look at ourselves and see ourselves for who we really are. When we see ourselves, then like Paul we will cry out, "Who shall deliver me from the body of this death?" (Romans 7:24).

If I keep living out of my body rather than my spirit, I'm going to die. My relationships will die. My finances are going to die. Everything is going to die as long as I keep living under the desires of my body. Who can get me out of my body and help me to live in my spirit? If I'm going to get help, it can't happen on Springer or 1-900-PSYCHIC.

My problems are so deep that only Jesus Christ our Lord has the answer. My problems are only going to be solved through Jesus Christ when I am in relationship with Him.

There is no longer any condemnation when you are in Christ Jesus. When you are in Him you will walk not after the flesh but after the Spirit. Satan has been doing a number on you. Like Simon, Satan desires to sift you like wheat. (Luke 22:31-32.) The good news is, Jesus has prayed for you that your faith will not fail. When you are strengthened then you can help others.

The sifting of wheat process presents a unique

parallel to Satan's scheme. The wheat is harvested, then placed on the threshing floor. Handfuls of wheat are shaken, then put on the floor. Pitchforks stab it, throw it up, watch it hit the floor and then stab it again. That process completed, the wheat goes into a teeter-totter box or a sifter. The box would shake side to side. Then the wheat is put back into the hand and is shaken some more.

You may feel you aren't able to praise God because the devil has you in his hands. That is what he has desired to do. He's got you in his hands, he's shaking you. He's throwing you and playing games with you. Once you get up he stabs you and throws you down again, and then he shakes you.

But I've made up in my mind. No longer am I going to be living under the flesh. I don't know about you, but I'm tired of the devil shaking me. I'm tired of the devil picking me up and throwing me down. I'm tired of the devil putting me in a box and shaking me. I've found out if I'm going to get help, I have to go to the Lord. Your help comes from the Lord. You cannot work your way out of it. You must turn it over to Jesus. Nothing is impossible with Him.

Jesus conquered sin and death when He took those keys from Satan two thousand years ago. Satan's only power comes when we give it to him, when we allow him to sift us because we have yielded to our flesh.

Thank God He delivered me. There is no mess that you're in that God can't pull you out of. Stop the struggle. Take back your dignity. The power of God lives in you.

7

The Pattern of Love

There are some books in the Bible that are very difficult to understand, and many people suggest that the book of Revelation is perhaps one of the most difficult. However, I believe the Song of Solomon is perhaps one of the most difficult books in the Bible to understand.

There used to be an R & B song, *Love Under New Management.* When a person is truly in love with God, that person finds sufficiency in God. They don't need God *and* somebody else. The one who wrote the song, *Love Under New Management,* was explaining that he had been disappointed in love and decided to change lovers or find one that he could surrender all to.

You may have experienced this kind of pseudoficial love in your live and now you have concluded that it's time to put your love under new management. You have come to recognize that you need to have God in your life in a greater way.

When God comes in your life in a greater way, it suggests some things. It suggests that you are complete in Him. No matter where I go, people know that I'm in love. It's without a doubt. When you're in love with Suzy or you're in love with Johnny, everybody knows that you're in love because there is a glow about you. There is something about you that lets them know you're in love. When you really love God, it ought to show up sometime. People should be able to look at you and say, "Wow, you're in love with somebody, aren't you?"

When you study the Word of God, understand that there are certain books in the Bible you have to read on two planes. Some books you have to really read from a literal perspective. Other books you have to examine from a figurative perspective. You have to look at a lot of symbolism in the Word of the Lord.

The Song of Solomon is a book with a lot of symbols, a lot of figurative language. You have to be able to interpret the symbolism. Let's find out now what the Word of God says. Let's examine this imagery, this symbolism, as God opens it up through the Holy Spirit.

> **I am the rose of Sharon, and the lily of the valleys.**
>
> **Song of Solomon 2:1**

He Is I AM

God deals with His I AM-ness. The I AM-ness of God has to do with the sufficiency of God. And the I AM-ness of God started in Exodus when Moses was getting ready to go to tell Pharaoh to let God's people go. Moses asked God, "Who should I tell them sent me?" And God said, "Moses, tell them that *I AM* has sent you."

Everything you need is in the I AM-ness of God. Jesus said later, "I am the way, the truth, and the life…" (John 14:6). "I am the good shepherd…" (John 10:11). "I am the light of the world…" (John 8:12).

When I understand the love of God, His I AM-ness answers all of my questions. Who's going to pay my bills? God says, I AM. Who's going to heal my body? Who's going to make a way out of no way? Who's going to heal my broken heart? God. Who's going to get me back in school next semester? Who's going to give me that promotion? God says, I AM. When I understand the I AM-ness of God, I don't need the I AM-ness plus you. The I AM-ness of God is the all-sufficiency of God.

He Is the Rose of Sharon

In the Song of Solomon, God is the rose of Sharon.

The rose symbolizes love. It is a flower symbolizing love. On the fourteenth of February many of you will be sitting at home waiting for somebody to give you a rose. If they give you a yellow rose, they're saying, "We're good friends." If they give you some red roses, they're saying they love you. God is the presence of the love in Sharon.

Now where was Sharon? Sharon was a fertile coastal land in Israel – a place where everything grew. It was a place of abundance so God said, "I am the rose." Or, "I am the love symbol in the midst of your place of abundance. While I am blessing you, while you are looking at all the abundance in your life," God says, "I am the rose. I'm in the midst of it." He doesn't want you to look at all the things and forget about Him. While He's blessing you, He keeps reminding you that all these things are possible because of the Rose.

When you get in your car, don't say, "Oh, I've got a nice car." You say, "There's a rose here." When you go in your house, say, "Oh, there's a rose here." The love of God is why you have the abundance in your life in the first place. God put the symbolism of love in the Word so we would not forget about the Blesser and simply focus on the blessings. Sometimes the more you get blessed, the quicker you forget about Him. God has to remind us that while He's blessing us, He is still the source of it and the source of our strength.

He Is the Lily of the Valley

He is also called the lily of the valley. The lily is a peculiar plant because in the midst of the valley, it is a good and fragrant thing in a low place. When a person goes into a valley, there are thickets and thorns, and all kinds of poisonous things. God stands out in the valley. He represents optimism in the midst of pessimism. He is the lily that represents the good in the midst of the bad. No matter how low your valley might be, He will constantly remind you that He is there.

The lily is symbolic of the presence of God in the midst of a dark and dreary place. The lily, a white plant, stands out among other plants in the field. And so God reminds us through His Word, that no matter what your valley looks like, He is going to rise up and show you that you're not going through it by yourself.

David said, "Yea, though I walk through the valley of the shadow of death . . . thou art with me . . ." (Psalm 23:4). How did David know that? Because God always reminded him of His presence. He always affirms His presence when I'm going through a valley: "You're not in that valley by yourself."

He represents His love to you in the midst of things that look like they are going to destroy you. He is your lily among thorns. Many of you have thorns all around you. You have thorns on your job and thorns in your home. God wants you to take your eyes off your problem, and start focusing on the positive rather than focusing in on the negative.

God calls us His daughters, symbolizing the birth of the Church. The *ekklesia* is you as feminine because Christ being the Bridegroom is coming back for the bride. The Church must be ready because she must birth things. Anyone who is in relationship with God will be productive (fertile). If you're not birthing anything, then you're probably not connected to the Lord.

He's the Apple Tree

As the apple tree among the trees of the wood, so is my beloved among the sons. I sat down under his shadow with great delight, and his fruit was sweet to my taste.

Song of Solomon 2:3

In a forest the apple tree is a rare find. God is that apple tree in the forest or the woods of our life. You have gone from tree to tree in your forest. You have looked for love here and you have looked for love there, but God offers you something you've never had before. His love is so different that you're going to look at all the other trees, and wonder why you spent time on other trees.

When you fall in love with God, everything else looks small. Solomon said that he sat down under his shadow. He was black. He had been working in the sun. He had labored in the vineyards of the people, but had neglected his own vineyards. He had given to everybody else, but had neglected himself. He had made everyone else's dreams come to pass, and he had given his love to everyone else but he was empty. God set him down under the shadow. God made him sit down.

There will come a time in your life when God is going to have you sit down. God will examine what you've been through and how you've lived your life for other people and how you've tried to work it out for everybody else. There will be a "come here and sit down" time.

That might be hard for you because you think you have all the answers. You've got all the solutions. You have the answer for everybody else, but God says if I'm going to bless you, you've got to sit down. That's what David meant in the 23rd Psalm when he said, "He maketh me to lie down in green pastures..." (v. 2). God will sit you down. There will be a time when God will cause you to do nothing but sit.

You are always trying to figure out what God is doing. You always think you can help God work it out, but He brings you to the apple tree of peculiar love and makes you sit down under it. And then He soothes you under the shadow because you have been in the sun. You have been laboring. You have been hurt. You are tired. God wants to minister to you. He wants to minister to you, give you the cool and comfort of His shadow -- His protection. So God, under the shade of His love, in the secret place of His tabernacle, will hide you. Sit down and let Him minister to you.

While you are sitting down doing nothing, you think that you're just marking time because you're not doing anything. There comes a period in everyone's life when God doesn't want you to do anything. You've worked. You have labored without purpose. Now He wants to minister to you. The first He ministers to you is by causing you to sit down. Then He puts you in the shade to soothe you from all the labor you've been through. He brings comfort to you.

He Is the Delightful Shade

Solomon was happy to be sitting down under the

shadow because God's fruit was sweet to his taste. He had been going from tree to tree in the forest. Some of the trees didn't even bear fruit. The ones that did bear fruit, the fruit was seasonal so the moment it fell from the tree, it rotted. And there was some other fruit. It was bitter. So he went from one bitter tree to a rotten tree, to a tree that didn't bear fruit.

Now God put Solomon under His tree, and everything that fell from that tree was sweet. Solomon knew the kind of love that got sweeter every day. Every day with Jesus is sweeter than the day before. He's giving me something new every day. This kind of satisfaction never gets old. Every day gets sweeter and sweeter.

This is what David meant in Psalm 34:8 when he said, "O taste and see that the Lord is good...." "Taste" symbolizes intimacy. As Solomon was being satisfied he was getting all he needed right there, in the shade, while God was ministering to him.

God sets me down and ministers to me and feeds me. He gives me sustenance and intimacy in the valley to strengthen me for the mountain climb ahead. You don't have strength because you go from one thing to another. You never spent any quality time sitting down, allowing God to minister to you, so you never have strength.

David said he waited patiently on the Lord. (Psalm 40:1.) When he did that, God encountered him, heard his cry and brought him up out of the miry clay, out of the horrible pit.

God has to feed me and set me down and minister to me to elevate me. He brings me to the banqueting house. God brings me to the place of spiritual buffet, a place of celebration. The banqueting house is symbolic of abundance. Every which way I turn I see a whole lot of stuff. So God says to you, "If you will sit down long enough and let me minister to you, then I will bring you to a place where you will have so many blessings. Every which way you turn, you will turn into blessings."

He Is Our Banner

There He puts His banner of love over you. The literal meaning of that is, God brought me to a place of abundance, then put a sign over me saying, "God's love." The figurative, spiritual implication is that God brought me to a place of abundance. People would know that it was God's love. So in the midst of all of my blessings, I've got to let people know that as God elevates me, it is because of God's love.

God delivered me from arrogant people who think what they have is because of them. They think because of the money or education they have that they are where they are. If you graduated summa cum laude or magna cum laude, it is because of the grace of God. I don't have time to ride around in my car with my nose all up in the air.

The banner of love is on me so everywhere I go, every elevation God takes me to, people are going to know that I love God and He loves me. So when I get ready to close on my new home, I'm going to say, "Excuse me, I've got to have a praise service." When I get ready to pay my tuition I will take time to let people know it was God. "Excuse me, y'all." When I get my new car, I have to testify that it was because of God. If you love Him like you say you love Him, that banner should show. Every time a blessing comes through, you need to say, "This is because of the love of God."

We get so sophisticated and arrogant when we are blessed. The reasons you can tell people who are blessed and arrogant is because you know they haven't spent time sitting down. But people who sat down under the tree, when they're blessed, everyone is going to know it was the love of God.

Read Romans, chapter 1. There you will find Paul's

testimony. "I am not ashamed of the gospel of Christ: for it is the power of God..." (v. 16). He understood that everything he possessed was because of God.

Every time I get out of my car, and I didn't have an accident, I thank God for His love. When you walk through the hospital you realize you have a lot to be grateful for.

Solomon said in the Song of Solomon 2:5 that he was sick of love. The Hebrew word here for "sick" is *chalah*. That means a flattering stroke. The love God gave Solomon was so great that he began looking at all his futile attempts to make people say they loved him and he realized he was sick of that kind of love. He was so complete in God that he didn't necessarily need anyone else to love him or affirm him.

We don't just experience love when we meet that special one. We should have love (the love of God) already when we meet them. When you understand the abundance of God's love, it makes no difference who comes in your life or out of your life. You've got another level of God that says, "I'm sick of earthly, fleshly love. I have so much love stored up in God that if someone leaves me, God will rock me in the midnight hour. If someone walks out on me, God will take care of me. God loves me so much it doesn't make any difference what someone says about me."

The reason why you'll just settle for anything is because you haven't fallen in love with God. When you understand how God loves you, you won't settle for anything else. It will take so much for me to have somebody now because God's love has put real love in its proper perspective. I don't look for the affirmations of other people now. I am so love sick. I'm in such an intimate relationship with Him.

He Supports Me with His Hands

God's left hand is under my head, and His right hand embraces me. The right hand symbolizes power. It symbolizes blessings. The Bible talks about how God is going to set to the right hand His sheep, to the left hand the goats. The left hand symbolizes condemnation. Look where God's left hand is. His left hand is under your head. His condemnation is under your head, and His blessing is on your body.

While He is embracing you, He has to constantly keep your mind in check so your ego will stay right. That's why Jesus was crucified on a hill called Golgotha which means the place of skulls because it was a crucifixion of the mind.

> I charge you, O ye daughters of Jerusalem, by
> the roes, and by the hinds of the field, that ye stir not
> up, nor awake my love, till he please.

Song of Solomon 2:7

Solomon is saying in this passage that God's hand is on him and no one should mess with him until God gets through doing His work. "In this season of my life, God is checking me and He's working on me. I don't need to be bothered right now. I don't need anyone right now because God is working on me."

There comes a point in your life when God is working on you and you don't need any interruptions. The problem is we start interrupting the process by allowing people to speak a word into our lives. Others try to tell us what God is doing, but God doesn't need any help. Don't disturb the process.

His Word Moves Circumstances

Learn to recognize when God is dealing with you. Learn to recognize the voice of God.

> The voice of my beloved! behold, he cometh
> leaping upon the mountains, skipping upon the hills.

Song of Solomon 2:8

Solomon tells us that it is the voice of the Lord that skips upon the mountain, that moves quickly. When you are in a love relationship with God, it is the voice of the Word of God that moves swiftly the moment you have an issue. God's Word is right there to solve the problem. The moment you have a question, the answer is right there. The moment you have a problem, the solution is right there. God's response time is so quick that before you can even get the question out, the answer is there.

The Father knows what things you have need of before you even ask. (Matthew 6:8.) So the moment you say, "God, I don't know how I'm going to pass this test," you hear, "I can do all things through Christ which strengtheneth me" (Philippians 4:13). You may say, "I don't know how I'm going to get healed," but you hear, "with His stripes I was healed." (Isaiah 53:5.) You might think, *I don't know how I'm going to work this thing out*, but God's Word reminds you, "And we know that all things work together for good to them that love God, to them who are the called according to his purpose" (Romans 8:28). The very moment I start getting problems out, God has the answer.

God Is Looking Into Your Situation

My beloved is like a roe or a young hart: behold, he standeth behind our wall, he looketh forth at the windows, shewing himself through the lattice.

Song of Solomon 2:9

Every now and then God will let me peek in to know He is still there. God looks through the lattice. I know there are times in your life when it seems like He is not there, but He is peeking at you. Sometimes you will go to church, and it seems like the Word of God was exactly for you. God was letting you know that He is right there in your circumstances. He will remind you of His presence.

If the relationship you are in has real sustenance, then you ought to be moving to higher levels. It should never be redundant or repetitive or stay at the same level. It has to have some value. It has to move you to different dimensions and challenge you to be better. You can do badly by yourself.

Now that you have sat under the tree, been fed and experienced the banqueting house, God does one more thing. You may be getting comfortable where you are but God wants to draw you into another dimension.

His New Dimension

Here's an invitation to a new situation. This invitation is to something better. You may still be dealing with some things that keep you from adequately appreciating the blessings. You just love the blessings, but now you must fall in love with the Blesser.

God longs to see if you love His blessings more than you love Him. So He asks you to leave the place of blessing. He may tell you to give your new car to somebody else. God may bless you with a brand new suit, then tell you to give it to someone who doesn't have a suit. Another season is coming now.

The winter is past. . . .

Song of Solomon 2:11

"Winter" in Hebrew is *estah*, meaning cloudy seas or stormy seas. He had you at the banqueting house and you were receiving blessings. You became connected to the blessings because that's what was affirming your value and your worth.

At the same time in your mind you were still having an internal storm because there were some things that people did to you in the forest. There were some people who wounded you. You still carry around that cold, bitter, winter experience. That was the cloudy season of your life, but God is getting ready to move you into another season.

Arise, my love, my fair one, and come away.
Song of Solomon 2:13

The earth and her glory are reminding you that a new season is getting ready to come in your life. The doves are flying and chirping. The flowers are sprouting up to let you know that God is taking you to a new season. It's one thing to move into a new blessing – a new mind-set. Even though you might be blessed and you might have the love of God, you still are going through a stormy season in your life because you haven't gotten over the wounds of your past. You haven't gotten over the problems and the issues that happened to you a long time ago. But God is getting ready to do a new thing in you – to make a better day in your life.

The winter is past. And the stormy season is gone. God is getting ready to do a new thing in your life. And so when you recognize the love of God and you start getting in love with Him and not the things, you start becoming submissive to the new thing that God is doing.

When the season starts changing, the heavens start declaring the glory of God. When you go through a cold winter, a bitter winter, you cannot wait for spring-time to come. Springtime represents new birth. And God says you've been through the winter too long, and now He is getting ready to birth something new in your life. He is getting ready to birth some dreams you've been waiting on.

That means all of those thoughts, all of those things people did to you are gone. All of that pain in your past is gone. All of that hurt is gone. It's a new day now so you don't have time to focus on that. Focus on what God is taking you into.

Stop focusing on what you came out of. Focus on what you are going into. When you thank God for what you're going into, you don't have time to complain about what folk did to you. It's a new day. He's doing a new thing. God wants to do something new in you because after He blesses you with things, He tests you to see what you are in love with. So don't act surprised when He blesses you and then asks you to give it up. Because if you give it up, He will bless you with more the second time than He did the first time. We've been guilty of going to God when we needed things only, but now we must declare our love for the Giver.

The winter is past. The rain is gone. The pain is gone. The hurt, the abuse, the violence are gone. Now you are moving into a new season, a new framework, a new paradigm, and a new mind-set that rises above the problem and says, "I'm satisfied in who God made me. I love God and He loves me. I don't need anyone else to affirm me because God loves me in spite of me. I don't have to impress anyone."

God is doing a new thing in you today. You are under new management.

8

Understanding Love

And one of the scribes came, and having heard them reasoning together, and perceiving that he [Jesus] had answered them well, asked him, Which is the first commandment of all?

And Jesus answered him, The first of all the commandments is, Hear, O Israel; The Lord our God is one Lord:

And thou shalt love the Lord thy God with all thy heart, and with all thy soul, and with all thy mind, and with all thy strength: this is the first commandment.

And the second is like, namely this, Thou shalt love thy neighbour as thyself. There is none other commandment greater than these.

Mark 12:28-31

The symbolism of Calvary depicts vertical and horizontal relationship. The vertical relationship is loving the Lord with all your heart, mind and strength. The horizontal is loving your neighbor as yourself. Jesus' crucifixion is suggestive of the fact that when our vertical relationship is right, our horizontal relationship will be healthy. And when Jesus Christ is in the center of that, all of our relationships will line up.

Many of us try to plant crosses horizontally. Crosses can't be planted horizontally. You must put it in the ground first. It has to be grounded. The symbolism here is, before I can really express or give love to somebody else, I first need to be grounded in the love of God. If someone is not in love with God, they cannot adequately love you.

The problem is, so many of us fall in love with people who don't love God. They are not qualified to love you, because how can they love you if they don't love God? God is the very standard by which I love you. We use the word "love" so loosely. We take the world's definition. The world says love is based on a feeling.

Biblical love has little to do with feelings and more to do with destiny. There are many days you wake up and you can't stand your spouse. It doesn't mean you don't love each other, you just don't want to talk today. You cannot use your feelings as the barometer to measure love, because what are you going to do when you don't *feel* loving? Just because you don't *feel* it doesn't mean you're not in love. Your love is not based on feelings, it's based on some factual information that is present in the Word of God. When you understand what love is, you're going to stop using that word so loosely.

First Corinthians, chapter 13, is our love guide. Jesus said the greatest commandment of all is love. It transcends all commandments. If you really work in God's love, all the other commands will line up in your behavior.

Three Kinds of Love

In the original Greek, there are three kinds of love: agape, phileo and eros, as I mentioned earlier in this text. Let's review them:

Agape. Agape is unconditional love. That's the love that God has for us.

Then there is *phileo.* That is the root word for Philadelphia, the city of brotherly love. Acts, chapter 1, is written to *Theophilus.* *Theo* means God, *philus* means love. Therefore Theophilus was a lover of God.

The third one is *eros,* the root word for erotica. That's relational love. Erotica love. Many of us see *eros* in the Bible, but *eros* in the Bible was never a physical deposit, it was always a spiritual deposit by God into Adam. Before Eve was even birthed, God placed *eros* in Adam so that when Eve was formed, when she was birthed, he already had *eros* for her. It was a spiritual attraction, not a physical one.

To Know You Is to Love You

You can probably count the people in your life who really know you. You count on one hand the people who genuinely want truth within you. Real love seeks to know you. Love doesn't want to get something from you. Love gives. Love wants to know you. When love really knows you, your good side and your bad side, love rejoices and accepts you for you. When you connect with that kind of love, there is freedom to be you. We're so afraid that if somebody really knew us, they would not love us.

The Lord numbers the hairs on your head. He knows every thought you have. He knows about your past. He knows about your future. He knows what you're thinking. He knows everything, yet He loves you. He knows me and He loves me in spite of me.

What we really want in love for our life is one that says, "I can accept your failures, I can accept your strengths, I love you based on who you are and not who people think you should be." I don't need love that will forsake me when times get rough. I need love that's for better or for worse, in sickness and health, for richer or for poorer.

You may not agree with this statement I'm about to make, but I believe this with all of my heart. *You can never fall out of love when you love biblically.* If you fell out of love, it was because you were loving physically. But true, authentic, spiritual, biblical love never fails. It never ever, ever fails.

Love Gives

John 3:16 says, "For God so loved the world, that he gave his only begotten Son..." Love brings something to me. Love deposits. God so loved that He gave. God demonstrated His love. Where my heart is, my treasure will be, so when I get the love of God in my heart, then my soul will inevitably belong to Him. The Word says if you believe in your heart and confess with your mouth the Lord Jesus, then you shall be saved. Salvation is of the heart and is spoken out of the mind. Therefore if I love God in my heart, then I'll love Him with my soul. When I love Him with my soul, I'm saved.

If someone is a good person, but they're not saved, it's evidence that they are not in love with God.

Someone recently told me, "I'm dating somebody who doesn't go to church, but he is a good person. He is not 'saved,' but he does good. He doesn't pay tithes, but he does give money to other people to help them out. He is a good person.

I said to the young lady, "Why doesn't he come to church?" She responded, "Well, I don't think he has to come to church to express his love to God." "Does he want to come to your house?" I asked. "Well, of course," was her reply.

If someone wants to come to your house, why wouldn't they want to go to God's house? They come to your house because they want to get something. We go to God's house because we want to get something. If you want to come to my house, then go to God's house with me first.

First Love

Whenever something gets on your mind, it controls you. You remember the very first time you were in love? You never forget that person's name. You think you are in love. When you are in love like that, they are constantly on your mind. You go to bed and they're on your mind. I used to go to class and she'd be on my mind. I'd write little notes, "Do you love me? Circle yes or no." I'd come home after school and get on the phone and talk to her for four or five hours. Why? Because she was on my mind. You tell your friends, "I'm in love. There she is."

Imagine if you had that kind of love for God. You would wake up with Him on your mind. You'd walk around all day with Him on your mind. You'd be telling folk about Him in your job, at school – you'd be constantly talking about Him. You would go to bed talking to Him. You wouldn't let anybody speak negatively about God or His Church. You would have an attitude.

I remember when I was on a basketball team in sixth grade. My girlfriend was a cheerleader and I was on the basketball team. I scarred my knee and it was bleeding, and it hurt, but I wasn't going to let her know it hurt. I got up and blew it off. I was acting like it wasn't hurting, because I didn't want her to know I was weak, because my love for her transcended my pain.

When you really love God and when He's on your mind, it doesn't make any difference what somebody does to you. It doesn't make any difference how bad it hurts, your love for Him transcends all the negative, all the pain, all the things that folks do to you. You'll be able to say like Paul:

> **For I am persuaded, that neither death, nor life, nor angels, nor principalities, nor powers, nor things present, nor things to come,**
>
> **Nor height, nor depth, nor any other creature, shall be able to separate us from the love of God. . . .**
>
> **Romans 8:38-39**

What's on your mind? Whatever is on your mind will control your body and your energies will be focused in that direction. Where your mind is, that is where your strength will be. Your mind will focus your energies in one particular direction. If you love God, all your energies are going to be focused toward giving Him glory. Everything you do in life is not for man but for God.

Love Yourself

I cannot adequately love you until I love myself. I meet people who don't love themselves, but they are always in love. You've got to love yourself. You may be saying, "Well, how do I love myself?" There are many ways you can love yourself. If you love yourself, your self-love is based on this one fact: "Let us make man in our image..." (Genesis 1:26). Then you know you are created in the image of God. Therefore you are

God's child. You have value because you are created in His image.

Now I never seek affirmation from man. I don't need a man or a woman to tell me how I look, how I'm doing or what I'm going to be like, because my wholeness is in God. When I take my one whole self, I'm looking for another whole person, so together we can make one whole unit. We think brokenness plus brokenness will make wholeness, but we simply have an egg with a crack in it.

I must use my love for myself as a standard by which I love others. When I do, I begin to say, "I love me too much to do that." "I love me too much to put up with that." "I love me too much to go through that." "I love me too much to have you move in with me." "I love myself too much to quit my job and let you take care of me." "I love me too much." "I love myself too much to let you pay for all this, because I know I'm going to have to pay you back."

The relationships you have expose how you feel and what you think about yourself. When somebody looks at you, they see who is in your life. They're looking at the statement your relationships are making about you. Woman of God, you come from a good family, good values and good morals. You grew up in a church,

Before You Say "I Do"

have a good job, and yet you hang out with some no church going, drug pushing, pants hanging off the behind, car bumping jerk. You are making a value statement about how you feel about yourself.

You may be a nice man with a good job and you have a good head on your shoulders, yet you hang out with a hoochie mama. Do you know why good girls like bad guys? Do you know why good guys like hoochie mamas? It is often an issue of control. If I am above that person I can manipulate them. The people you have in your life are reflections of how you feel about yourself.

Just for a moment I want you to think about the five closest people to you. What is their presence in your life saying about you? Many of us fall in love for all the wrong reasons. We're searching for affirmation. The greatest love you will ever have in your life is Jesus Christ. When all the women have hurt you and all the men have hurt you, Jesus will be right there. He'll be there in the midnight hour to dry your tears.

I'm in love with another man and there is nothing strange or off about it. His name is Jesus. It's time to get in a relationship with the love of your soul. It's time to circle *yes* on that little note to Jesus. It's time to start

118

talking to Him like you've been talking to that person on the phone.

Before you say "I do," make these principles your priority.

1. Learn to love the One who will never leave you or forsake you. (Hebrews 13:5.) Refuse to love anyone more than you love God.

2. Learn to love yourself. You are created in God's image.

3. Identify the culprit. The devil is subtle. Learn to listen to the right voice, God's voice.

4. Have the proper covering. Look for and allow God's covering to be your example.

5. Be careful in your communication. Watch what you say and who you say things to. Share your heart's desires and dreams with God. He can be trusted.

6. Don't compromise God's commandments. Allow the *yes* of God to be your *yes* and His *no* to be your *no*.

The first one you must say "I do" to is God. If He is not your first love, then no other love on this earth will ever be right for you.

Before you walk down that aisle to say "I do," be sure you have already said "I do" to the supreme example of love – Jesus Christ.

About the Author

Bishop Joseph Warren Walker, III was born in Shreveport, Louisiana, on July 28, 1967, to Deacon Joseph W. Walker, Jr. and Rosa H. Walker. He was educated at Fair Park High School in Shreveport. He received his B.A. from Southern University in Baton Rouge, his Master's of Divinity from Vanderbilt and a Doctorate of Ministry from Princeton Theological Seminary, all with honors.

Bishop Walker was baptized, licensed and ordained in the Mount Canaan Baptist Church of Shreveport, Louisiana, where Dr. Harry Blake serves as pastor. He has served in many capacities. He has served as campus minister for the Baptist Student Union at Southern University. He has served as General Overseer of College Ministries for the Full Gospel Baptist Church Fellowship. Presently, he serves on the Bishops' Council of the Full Gospel Baptist Church Fellowship and is the Bishop of Evangelism.

Foremost, he is the pastor of the Mount Zion Baptist Church of Nashville, Tennessee. He began his pastorate in the spring of 1992 with 175 members and presently the ministry has grown to over 6,000 and continues to grow at a phenomenal rate of over 1,000 souls a year. Mount Zion has grown to six weekly services in three locations. Under his leadership, the church is presently engaged in the completion of a $12 million ministry complex, which is the first phase of a $30 million twelve-year project. His weekly television and daily radio ministry bless thousands of people across the world.

He is the President and CEO of J. W. Walker Ministries and the President of Exodus Production, Inc. He serves as adjunct professor of Religion at Tennessee State University and is the author of *From Tragedy to Triumph*. He is a member of several organizations, including the Omega Psi Phi Fraternity, Inc. He has received numerous awards and has been featured in several publications. Bishop Walker is married to Dr. Diane G. Walker, DDS. He is an anointed man of God for such a time as this.

Product List

JWW - 10104   "From Poverty to Prosperity"

                                            4-tape series - $20

JWW - 10105   "Love, Relationships and Marriage"

                                            4-tape series - $20

JWW - 10107   "From Tragedy to Triumph"

                                            4-tape series - $20

JWW - 10108   "How to Deal with Heart Trouble"

                                            2-tape series - $10

JWW - 10109   "Names of God"

                                            2-tape series - $10

JWW - 10110   "The Ministry of the Holy Spirit"

                                            4-tape series - $20

JWW - 10112   "Divine Dollars and Spiritual Sense"

                                            4-tape series - $20

JWW - 10113   "Living for the City"

                                            2-tape series - $10

JWW - 10114   "Miracles"

                                            4-tape series - $20

For an additional listing of sermons and visions
log onto our website at:

www.jwwministries.com